ROMAN POLITICAL IDEAS AND PRACTICE

F. E. ADCOCK

ROMAN POLITICAL IDEAS
AND PRACTICE

Ann Arbor Paperbacks
The University of Michigan Press

Jerome Lectures   Sixth Series

PREFACE

THE LECTURES that appear as the chapters of this book were delivered on the Thomas Spencer Jerome Foundation at the University of Michigan in October 1957 and again at the American Academy in Rome in February and March 1958. In revising them for their second delivery and then for publication I have sought to profit from the criticisms of friends and the opportunity of including my own second thoughts. They contain, as they are bound to do, many judgments on which there is not, or likely to be, agreement between students of the topic with which they are concerned, and this is particularly true as regards the interaction of practice and ideas. To deploy at length the ancient evidence and the many long-drawn controversies which the topic has provoked would require a volume which would exceed the purposes of the Jerome Foundation. But I have referred to those passages from ancient authors which are of especial importance and have indicated my debt to modern scholars on particular topics whether my debt to them resulted in agreement or, more rarely, in disagreement with their views.

For the high distinction of appointment to the Jerome lectureship, I wish to express my thanks to the committee of the Foundation. The task of preparing and delivering these lectures has been a very pleasant one, and I have many reasons to be grateful to scholars in the University of Michigan and in particular to Dean Ralph A. Sawyer and Professor Arthur Boak for many acts of kindness, notable even in that most hospitable seat of learning. The fortunate provision that the lectures are also delivered at the American Academy in Rome enabled me to spend a period of residence there among old and new friends, during which I owed much to the Director, Lawrence P. Roberts and to Herbert Bloch, the Professor in charge of the School of Classical Studies. I would be glad to think that with these lectures I have been able to make some partial repayment for the happiness I enjoyed both in Ann Arbor and in Rome.

My friends at Cambridge, G. T. Griffith and A. H. McDonald, have done me the service of reading proofs as well as of making valuable criticisms and suggestions at various stages of the preparation of the lectures. For errors of fact or doctrine I must accept the responsibility, but these would have been more numerous and serious had it not been for their help.

King's College   F. E. A.
Cambridge
January 1959

CONTENTS

ROMAN POLITICAL IDEAS AND PRACTICE

I

EARLY ROME

THIS BOOK will attempt to make Roman political ideas and practice throw some light upon each other down to the time when the Principate that had succeeded to the Republic, as the Republic had succeeded to the Monarchy, was by way of reverting to undisguised and uninhibited autocracy, under which politics really ceased to exist.

The historical process during this whole period has a kind of continuity. But this is not so much due to logic or political speculation as to the practical adaptation to events of certain ideas which are really ingrained habits of mind and character, in general conservative, but capable of change and even of innovation. This fact will, I hope, justify an element of narration here and there, needed to make clear not only what happened but how it happened, which, if Ranke is to be believed, is the purpose of historical study.

I begin with Early Rome, and with its whereabouts. For while geography rarely decides the fate of communities, it rarely fails to affect it. The river Tiber had its share in making Rome what it was. As poets were to complain, the stream of the river ran strongly towards the sea. The mouth of the Tiber was only some twenty miles away, but the voyage from its mouth to the site of Rome was hard going for primitive ships.[1] In the *Aeneid* it took a miracle to get them there.[2] While Athens with its harbour of the Piraeus, or London or New York, is bound, in a measure, to look out to sea, Rome looked out to the land and the Romans were, above all, a land people. They loved the land—their own and that of their nearest neighbours—they were instinctively distrustful of the sea. The sea, after all, had a quite un-Roman changeability of mood. When it was rough, it was rough, and when it was smooth, it was only waiting to be rough. The poet Lucretius is never more Roman than when he speaks of the "treacherous allurements of a calm sea."[3]

In the next place, the Tiber was not easy to cross, but where Rome was to stand, there was an island which helped a crossing, and it was just here that the small communities of shepherds or farmers that were to coalesce into Rome gravitated towards each other from either side of the river. And this mattered. For the site of Rome became the meeting place of two racial groups, the one Latin from the south, the other Sabine from the north. As these two groups became fused together, they assumed the hard-wearing quality which, throughout early history, seems to be not infrequently vouchsafed to mixed peoples of strains that are not too diverse. The fortunes of Rome were to be more closely linked with her Latin kinsmen, but the Sabine element, smaller as it doubtless was, added a sturdy masculine and old-fashioned virtue which was still claimed for the Sabines by the Romans at a time when they could not so easily claim it for themselves.[4]

Apart from this effect of the fusion of two land peoples, what matters is that the Romans were, above all, peasants, racy of the soil, with the mental make-up of peasants which for centuries they never wholly lost.[5] Of their great poems, the one that is most Roman in spirit is the *Georgics*—the epic of the farmer. Herein, in their peasant character, lies a secret of their institutions and ideas in politics, and, indeed, in much beside.

The process by which the people who lived where Rome was to stand coalesced is illustrated by signs of the alliance of two groups. This alliance ended in complete fusion, and with it we may first speak of Rome as a city-state and of a Roman constitution with political elements.

The political institutions of the Romans before the establishment of the Republic are, in the main, a matter of conjecture. This indeed they were when the ancient tradition about them took shape. It is not even certain that Tacitus was speaking the precise truth when he began the *Annals* with the categorical statement that the city of Rome was from its beginning in the hands of kings "Urbem Romam *a principio reges habuere*" but it is beyond reasonable doubt that, however the earliest Roman city-state was governed, the Republic was preceded by a period of monarchy. This Monarchy, in its latest phase at least, was in the hands of an alien Etruscan dynasty. Whatever their origin (a topic on which I need not pronounce) the Etruscans were, or had become, an aristocratic caste of warriors of greater military skill than their neighbours, open to outside influences in the arts of war and of peace. They were, in fact, not unlike the medieval Normans who carved out their principalities in South Italy and Sicily. Towards the close of the seventh century, or perhaps a trifle later, they mastered Rome and imposed themselves on a Latin-Sabine community which had by now already developed regal institutions. It may be asserted with confidence that when Rome was ruled by kings their kings enjoyed, or had come to enjoy, the plenary and comprehensive powers which were summed up in the word *imperium*,[6] the most significant word in the vocabulary of Roman constitutional statecraft. It is more than possible that the powers of the kings reached their most absolute form under the Etruscans, and that the insignia of regality as, for instance, the *fasces*, of

Etruscan origin if in name Latin,[7] accompanied the final development of this power.

The Monarchy was in origin not hereditary; and it was not really limited or constitutional. The choice of the king needed to be accompanied by signs of the good will of Heaven, but the kings of Rome were not divinely appointed—they were not vice-gerents of a god and they were not regarded as in any sense divine. The king was not a magistrate in the sense that he was elected by the People and charged with the execution of the People's will. The *imperium* which he possessed was unlimited in range, he was "over all persons and in all causes supreme". He possessed the *auspicia,* the means of testing the will of the gods, whose favour had approved his choice as king and so, in a sense, guaranteed his power. Thus he had the high duty of securing the peace of the gods, the *pax deorum* which was needed for the safety and prosperity of the community both in war and in its peasant activities. For the gods might send misfortune on your arms and blight upon your fields. So far he was priest. In war the king had unfettered, undivided command and if anyone acted for him, it was as his deputy by his free choice. Thus he was general, and the *imperium* had a military character which it never lost. He was also the fountain of justice, the source of right. If he permitted the people a say in judgment it was by *his* grace and not their *right* or the *right* of the man who was being judged. For neither the people as a whole nor any citizen had any positive right that limited the king's *imperium*. Thus he was priest, general and judge by virtue of this indivisible *imperium,* which comprehended all the functions of whatever kind that were needed to rule the community, in which the People was not sovereign but rather obedient to his will. Such was the *imperium* which the Republic inherited as the vehicle of rule. *Regere imperio* had been the practice and the business of the *rex*, as, to Virgil,[8] it was the practice and the business of the Roman People. So much for the kings.

Within the Roman community the absolutism of the king was paralleled, though not limited, by the absolutism of the father of the family, the *pater familias*, who exercised undisputed rule over his wife, his children, and his household. In the Roman community there had arisen aristocratic families which were admittedly superior in power or prestige or in birth to the other families. The fathers, the *patres,* who ruled over these aristocratic families could be summoned by the king to give him the benefit of their wise counsel. But the king was not bound to be guided by them: they did not limit his power. They were authoritarian themselves in their homes, and they would not be reluctant to accept as natural the authoritarian position of the king. These advisers were the oldest members of their families and so this concourse of elders had the name of Senate.

As has been said, Rome had enjoyed or endured a short series of alien Etruscan kings, whose *imperium* was perhaps more absolute, if not more comprehensive, than that of their predecessors. They had brought to Rome some of the civilization which the Etruscans had bought or borrowed from Greek artists or initiated themselves. As the sixth century drew to its close Rome began to look like any other centre of Etruscan power, and began, indeed, to encroach on the lands of its Latin neighbours. But that was not destined to continue. The Etruscans remained as alien as they were few in number. Their dynasty broke with the Roman aristocracy. A rising drove them from Rome and though there was a brief revival of Etruscan power, Rome became a wholly Roman State again not later than the beginning of the fifth century B.C.

In saying this I am following the orthodox tradition. In doing so, I provisionally reject the conclusions recently advanced by distinguished Swedish scholars, who deduce from the results of their excavations that Rome did not become a Republic until the middle of the fifth century[9] and who believe Rome did not really settle down as one for several decades more.[10] The effects of their conclusions on the tradition are very formidable, and I do not expect they will succeed in proving their case beyond doubt. But if they do, the general doctrine of this chapter survives pretty well intact, apart from a shift in chronology. Anyhow, at some time or other, the Monarchy was replaced by a Republic. Politically, royal autocracy became anathema, though the Latin title of king was allowed to describe the man who exercised some religious functions that had been the duty of the kings. But what does matter is that the Republic carried over the root ideas of the pre-Etruscan community in Rome.

The tremendous powers of the *imperium* were not challenged by the revolution that overthrew the Etruscan dynasty, but it is *a priori* improbable that there was not some safeguard against the return of monarchy by way of the *imperium*. A series of *interreges* whose tenure of power was limited to a few days was plainly no lasting solution, though it might tide over an interruption of power or even the transition from monarchy to Republic. For the Republic to use the traditional all-embracing power of the *imperium* without risking its freedom from monarchy the first natural remedy was to provide for the extinction of a man's *imperium* after a settled period of time, viz. a year; a second safeguard was the presence during that year of an *imperium* equally powerful, held by another parallel magistrate. One way to avoid monarchy, the rule of one, is to have dyarchy, the rule of two, and to have it from the start.

It is therefore reasonable to accept the tradition, or perhaps the deduction, of the Romans, that the Republic began with two supreme magistrates, equal and possibly opposite, a combination which could not serve the ambitions of one magistrate without the self-abnegation of his partner. The very comprehensiveness of the *imperium* meant that each of the two magistrates rivalled the other, and neither could prevail over the other, for both had power that was all-pervading.

This overlapping of the two comprehensive powers of two equal magistrates could be represented by the doctrine that where they disagreed the magistrate who denied action prevailed over the magistrate who initiated it. Whether the doctrine itself was formulated at the beginning of the Republic or not, the fact that each of the two magistrates provided a check on the other was visible. But the Romans were well aware of what follows when an irresistible force meets an immovable mass, and you cannot promote obstruction into a system. So if the safety of the community required the unfettered power of one man, then *for an emergency*—with the extreme limit of six months—the two chief magistrates made way for the even more regal *imperium* of an officer, a dictator or, to use an older title, a *magister populi*, who was named with due solemnity by one of the two magistrates. This officer was superimposed on the regular magistrates, he was not limited by the existence of any comparable *imperium*, and he himself appointed a lieutenant, the Master of the Horse (*magister equitum*), who owed him obedience and disappeared with the dictator who appointed him. Thus by what has been called a paradox of genius the Romans contrived to preserve the absolute efficacy of the *imperium* while providing safeguards against the dangers of lasting disunion through plurality and of lasting autocracy through indivisibility.

The Senate continued to advise the executive without controlling it, for, as under the Monarchy, its advice was there for the executive to follow or not as it thought well, and it was only given when the magistrates asked for it.

There now remains the People, the *Populus Romanus,* which had a history of its own even before the fall of the Monarchy. It had been the combination of a number of families organized into units based on birth, the *curiae.* At a late stage in the Monarchy as Roman territory was extended new Romans were created by the absorption of a wider population into the citizen body. It was the first great manifestation of the Roman instinct for assimilation.[11] The purpose of this later creation was to strengthen the State by a liberal adoption into rights in return for service to the community, especially in war.[12] Thus the organization was in terms of military units—the centuries. The old order by *curiae* did not disappear; it had some functions, and it approved the *imperium* of the regular chief executive. But the Republic, no less than the Monarchy, needed the support of all its citizens whether they belonged to the *curiae* or not, and the community embraced all Romans, the *Populus Romanus.* The interest of the Roman People was the one overriding care of the all-powerful executive and the all-wise Senate. The Republic, the *res publica,*[13] the public affair, could be reasonably paraphrased by Cicero[14] as the *res Populi,* the People's affair.

This now was the Roman State—the People of Rome, as the Athenian State was the Athenians, the Lacedaemonian State the Lacedaemonians, and as what is briefly called the United States is the People of the United States.

Besides the *imperium* in the plenitude of its efficacy, there was another idea which may be regarded as a heritage from the Etruscan rulers. The Etruscans had marked off their cities

not only by material defences but by the sacred definition of
the area which was under the especial protection of the gods.
This practice was followed at Rome. Within this area the
community was in a peculiar sense at home, and the area was
so defined by the word *domi* 'at home'.[15] The word did not
define the whole territory of the community; this had the
name of the landed possession of the Roman People, the *ager
Romanus*, which attests the peasant character of the community.
More than that, whatever lay outside the domestic area was
described as the field of warfare, *militiae;* this word *militiae*
attests the soldierly activity of the community outside the
rule of peaceful law and custom which lay within the sacred
boundary of the city itself. Here, in the field of warfare,
the magistrate vested with the *imperium* exercised it with the
autocratic rigour accepted by Roman discipline. Within the
city he wears the dress of peace, his lictors have not the axes
in their *fasces;* great as is his authority he wields it as a citizen
among citizens. When, as will be seen later, the commons
chose men to give them protection, these men limit their
activity to the city and do not intervene outside its precincts.
And, by parity of reasoning, when the Roman People meets as
an army for the appointment of the magistrates who will
command them in the field, they meet, not within the sacred
bounds of the city but outside it in the field named after Mars,
the war-god of the community.

I have just spoken of the *ager Romanus*, the land where
Romans lived. As the community extended its borders, this
territory was divided into tribes. In the more primitive State
there had been three tribes called Tities, Ramnes and Luceres,
names which almost certainly reflect ethnic elements.[16] These
had given place to tribes which were local in the sense that
four of them contained those citizens who lived in the city and

so were called "urban", and an increasing number of "rustic" tribes. The sixteen earliest of these were named after old aristocratic families, which were, it may be assumed, the largest or most powerful landowners in each of them. As Roman territory grew and grew, new tribes with geographical names were added to these, until finally, in the third century B.C., the total number was thirty-five. This process reflected the peasant character of the community, and as the tribes came to be political divisions of the plebeians and then of the whole Roman People, they had, as will be seen later, an effect on the balance of urban and agrarian elements in the citizen body.[17] But wherever Romans came to live, as the Monarchy and then the Republic extended its borders, the heart of the body politic was, and always remained, in Rome itself. Granted this strong bond of unity, what does the State mean to the Romans?

To judge from the nuances of language, the State had not, to the early Romans, an emotional tinge like "the country", "the Fatherland", or "*la patrie*"—it was *Res Publica*. The emotional concept of the *patria* is not attested for Rome until the Republic had existed for some three hundred years.[18] As we may accept Cicero's interpretation—that *res publica* was *res populi*, so we may accept Cicero's matter-of-fact definition of *populus* as the union of a number of men associated by the two bonds of common acknowledgment of right and the common pursuit of advantage or interest.[19] The idea is not racial, not mythological, not ideological: it is practical. To the ordinary Roman, the *res publica* was, in practice, the business of the people, their right and their interest. The active promotion of this right and interest to which Romans must devote themselves demanded more than devotion, it demanded capacity, competence, experience and knowledge. These qualities were most at home in the ranks of the nobles, and so it was in the national interest that these—the nobles—should rule. This ingrained belief in aristocracy was not so much sentimental as prudential in origin, and it was very durable. The counterpart of this popular belief in the Roman aristocracy was the Roman aristocracy's belief in itself.

The political or military guidance of the national interest received no material reward. But it received the public recognition of high office in the State, which conferred on the recipient what the Romans called *dignitas,*[20] the quality which marks out the great man from the small. The small man did not claim *dignitas,* but he did claim what his citizenship gave to him, that is *libertas.*[21] This was not freedom to do whatever he would, but to do what law and custom allowed him to do, and at the same time, not to suffer more than law and custom allowed him to suffer. The *dignitas* of the great man did not, or should not, deny the *libertas* of the small man. The historian Livy compendiously describes a Roman gentleman of the old school as one who was "as mindful of the *libertas* of others as he was of his own *dignitas*".[22] The small man was tenacious of his *libertas,* the great man was more than tenacious of his *dignitas,* which was linked with his pride in his family and was enhanced by office and the service of the State. The claim of *dignitas* is indeed the most constant ingredient in the active political history of the Republic.

In this context there is another idea of lasting importance in Roman public affairs. A Roman entrusted with the care of the public interest was expected to pursue it conscientiously, single-mindedly, and honourably. The concept that embodied this expectation was *fides.*[23] When the Senate suggested that a magistrate should act, it added the phrase that he should act as seemed good to him in accordance with the national interest and his own *fides.*[24] It was the constant reminder of that sense

of duty and scruple that the community expected to find in
its leaders. The same idea, it may be added, governed the
relation of a powerful Roman to clients who had placed themselves under his protection.[25] The clients have no claim in law,
but as they trust him, so he must deserve and earn their trust.

Granted the ideas of aristocratic obligation by *fides* and the
aristocratic claim of *dignitas*, we may credit the early Roman
community with an assessment of men. This may result in
their admitted possession of what was called or came to be
called 'authority' (*auctoritas*).[26] This word implied that some
people by virtue of their wisdom, their position, their natural
force of character, their achievements, their family tradition,
or some combination of these, were expected to give a lead
which others should follow. Such people as these possessed
auctoritas; and the Senate, which so largely consisted of just
such people, might possess a kind of corporate *auctoritas*. This
idea reinforced the Romans' instinct for accepting inequality
once a certain minimum of right and *libertas* was assured. The
Romans did not ever believe in what has been called parity of
esteem, and they no more believed that all men were equally
suited to govern the State than that all men were equally tall.
To suppose that a man who had led armies or guided the
counsels of the community with courage and wisdom was not
superior to a man who had done neither would have seemed
to a Roman weak-minded credulity. And where a man possessed *auctoritas,* backed by *fides*—which meant that *auctoritas*
would not be misused—the Romans did not need to be persuaded, or to know why he held this or that opinion. With a
great economy of time and mental exertion, they were content
to be guided by him. And to this they added an aptitude for
discipline, which was the main ingredient in their military
quality, and marked them off from almost all other ancient
peoples.

In this military context there is another side to this matter which reflects the lasting character of the Romans. No people have surpassed the Romans in over-all success in war. But I cannot remember any glorification of war in such Latin literature as I have read. "To drink delight of battle" would have seemed to the Romans a form of intoxication, and they regarded war, like any other serious job of work, as best done sober. Like all sensible men, they thought peace better than war, but also, like most sensible men, they thought victory better than defeat. They lost many battles, but in almost all their wars there was one battle they made sure of winning—the last one. And when it came to making peace the Romans were, in most of their early history, as wisely reasonable in victory as they were indomitable in defeat. It was this moderation which, when their power prevailed more and more in the Mediterranean world, seemed to others and indeed to themselves one secret of their success.

And, finally, in their native conception of religion there was a strong prudential element. The worship of the gods of the State, particularly that of Jupiter Best and Greatest on the Capitoline, was, above all, directed to preserving the *pax deorum,* which means continuing good relations between Heaven and the Roman community, and to observing in good time any sign of divine disfavour. It was formal and formalistic, perhaps increasingly so under Etruscan influence, a matter of correctness and of scruple rather than of emotion or faith, of punctual performance of obligations, a species of honest diplomacy between earth and Heaven. (The days of chicaneries and ingenuities that use religious forms for political purposes were still far in the future.) When in the Middle Republic the Romans claimed that their piety was a main source of their advance to power,[27] they meant by piety a collection of respectable qualities joined together by a conscientious punc tiliousness. And they rightly judged that their way of behaving towards Heaven was a suitable and profitable way of behaving to their fellow citizens and to their allies. They deduced from their religion that war required the sanction of a good and sufficient cause and they were careful to convince themselves that they had left nothing undone to satisfy themselves and the gods that their action was just or at least correct. And this conviction was reinforced by a peasant's belief that he should not leave his farm and go to war unless Heaven was kind to it in his absence.[28]

Besides the care to placate the greater gods, the primitive peasant community of Rome had its nearer gods that personified the accidents of life or the forces of Nature that might do good or harm to their fields and their crops. (Had the primitive Romans ridden bicycles, they would, I imagine, have had a domestic goddess named *Punctura.*) These, too, were appeased, if need be, by a species of sympathetic magic. When the red rust (*robigo*) endangered your crops, you sacrificed a red dog, and so on. It was of the same pattern, the same revelation of the peasant mind, as true for the *pater familias* at his altar or at his hearthstone as for the king and his successors in the temples of the State.

It was all summed up in the word *religio,* the bond of obligation, which is imposed as duty on the citizen and binds him to the gods.

Such were the ideas—of *auctoritas, dignitas* and *libertas,* the idea of *fides* towards men and of *religio* towards gods, the conception of the comprehensive *imperium* in the two spheres *domi* and *militiae*—which we may assume governed ethical and political thought when the Roman Republic came into being.

It will be observed that these ideas are not, in essence, due to adventures of the intellect—which is what we often predicate of ideas—they lie near to the springs of action; they reflect an instinctive attitude towards the Roman's gods, his rulers and himself. And they are associated with what may be called qualities, such as *gravitas,* which befits the possessor of *auctoritas* or *dignitas; pietas,* which manifests at once an addiction to *religio* and a sense of family solidarity. The quality of *virtus,* an ingrained manly courage, belongs to the ethic of the soldier and is the ally of *disciplina,* and this last was taught to the Roman by the strong tradition of obedience which belonged to the family. Here it was inculcated by the unquestioned absolutism in the home of the *pater familias,* which was then accepted as belonging to the holder of the *imperium.* And with such ideas and qualities the Roman Republic was knit together. Finally, there was something for which it is hard to find in Latin a single descriptive word, what we would call a conservative belief that the way of their forebears—the *mos maiorum*—was a norm of action which did not need at the outset the protection of statutes. The burden of proof lay on those who would vary this and do something differently, and the degree of variation was made to seem as slight as possible. But in the field of war the Romans were willing to learn from their enemies, and in their other characteristic activity, the building of a private law, they moved forward with caution and circumspection. But, in general, they would subscribe to the dictum that when it is not necessary to change, it is desirable not to change. And they were apt to give to what was familiar the benefit of the doubt. And so I will conclude this chapter with a pleasing example of this frame of mind which is recorded by the elder Pliny[29] on the good authority of no less a scholar than Marcus Terentius Varro. In what is for us the year 263 B.C. the consul Manius Valerius took the Sicilian city of Catania, and sent the town's sundial to Rome to be put up in the Forum. Catania lies three degrees east of Rome. As Pliny says, the sundial's markings did not match the hours. But the Romans went by it for ninety-nine years, until at last the censor Quintus Marcius Philippus put up an accurate sundial by its side, apparently leaving the old one where it stood.

II

THE GROWTH
OF THE REPUBLIC

BY THE TIME the Republic had replaced the Monarchy the Roman People comprised two elements, the one patrician, the other plebeian. The idea that these elements were of different racial origins is now generally abandoned. There was a difference, but it was, so far as one can see, social rather than racial in character. The patricians consisted of the members of *gentes* which had come to claim privilege of birth and aristocratic tradition reflected in institutions, such as form of marriage, which the plebeians did not share. The differentiation between them may have been strengthened by the aristocratic character of the Etruscans, and the Etruscan kings of Rome may have found in the Roman aristocracy a support of their power, and later sought to strengthen both the State and their hold upon it by enlisting the plebeians in the army.[1] But their autocracy in the end combined against them the patrician claim to *dignitas* and the plebeian claim to *libertas*: they outstayed their welcome and the Monarchy was overthrown.

Its fall brought to the Romans freedom but not equality of status. The leadership and direction of the community passed, in general at least, to members of the patrician *gentes* and to the Senate which represented them through the elders of the aristocratic families. It is roughly true to say that while the patricians had become more exclusive, the plebeians had become more inclusive in the regal period, as the size of the community increased by immigration and territorial expansion.[2] It may be assumed that the plebeians, to begin with, became self-conscious through the common possession of a religious centre which was served by their earliest officers, the *aediles*. Even before the advent of the Republic the plebeian body had included men brought into the Roman community as the Monarchy had extended its borders. It had become diverse in character, comprising independent peasants or artisans in Rome and its neighbourhood, men who had placed themselves as clients under the protection of patricians and owed loyalty to their patrons, some, perhaps, who had stood in a like relation to the kings, and, finally, members of the lesser gentry who had not risen to rank with the patricians, however near they had come to it. It is important to realize that within the plebeian body there was this natural diversity of interests which might come to have a political effect. The patrician body, on the other hand, was united in tradition and social consciousness; small as it was, by its military and landowning character and its clientele it went far to justify the position of privilege which it enjoyed.

The problems that faced the Early Republic were not simple problems; it is instructive to observe how they were solved by the application to them of the instinctive statecraft that seemed to be ingrained in the Roman character and by a sturdy common-sense that waited upon the essential patriotism of the early Roman community.

The revolution which overthrew the Monarchy was, it may be assumed, initiated by the Roman aristocracy, with the concurrence at least of the mass of the Roman People.[3] So far, so good. But it was not enough to cease to be a monarchy: the new freedom had to be made secure, and the new constitution had to be geared to the needs of the State. The position of Rome among her neighbours was precarious: we may fairly suppose that she was faced with the hostility or suspicion of neighbouring Etruscan powers because of her present independence, and of her Latin kinsmen and neighbours because of her past activity as a centre of Etruscan territorial ambition. Hard fighting and shrewd policy averted disaster. It is more than possible that some non-patricians were accepted as magistrates in these difficult times.[4]

The new Republic came to terms with her Latin and Hernican neighbours and this triple alliance faced her enemies, Volsci, Aequi and Etruscans, on three fronts. The patricians had already closed their ranks against immigrants of their own class,[5] the last-comers probably being the Claudian family of Sabine origin.[6] They now formed a closed body and sought with almost complete success to monopolize the executive under the leadership of the Fabian house. The patrician nobles may have tried for a time to meet the military needs of the state by the use of their own retainers or clients but, if so, this phase ended with the destruction of the Fabii and their followers in a great disaster on the river Cremera.[7] We may suppose that there was a military reform or, more probably, a return to the mobilization of as many citizens as could equip themselves to fight in the line of battle. The army of the centuries became, precisely when is a matter of dispute, the most responsible Assembly of the Roman people, replacing, for most purposes, an Assembly of *curiae,* the earliest units of the Roman community. The Assembly of the Centuries retained its military organization and was so arranged that political power rested most with those who could make the most effective military contribution. This they would do by equipping themselves to fight in the front ranks of the citizen phalanx or as cavalry or, more probably, mounted infantry *d'élite.*

But by now the patricians had become a plainly dominant

order in the State. Though the Senate will have admitted to its
deliberations any non-patricians who had attained high office,
as indeed could hardly be avoided, the patricians, who formed,
at least, the very great majority of senators, claimed to themselves a special position *vis-à-vis* the People. First, when, as
might happen, the chief executive was removed by the chances
of war or any other cause, the *auspicia,* so it was said, returned
to the *patres,* that is to the patrician members of the Senate, and
they by the use of *interreges* provided for the transition to new
magistrates. And second, the *patres* asserted a claim to pronounce upon the validity of such decisions as the Assembly of
Centuries might make. These might become effective through
the initiative of a magistrate taking the advice of the Senate in
advance, or by an act of patrician members of the Senate con-
firming the validity of the Assembly's decision. Thus in terms
of political power the closed body of patricians became as it
were a state within the state, with special rights protected by
custom if not conferred by statute, and no doubt a strong
corporate sense. But in return they presently accepted the
existence of a parallel to themselves in the shape of the plebeians, who elected from their own number leaders who were
called the Tribunes of the Plebs. These asserted a claim to protect plebeians from hard usage by patrician magistrates or
patrician judges by an admitted right of help (*auxilium*).[8]

The organized meetings of the plebeians in what was called
their *Concilium* could pass resolutions about their own affairs
which were recorded by their own officers. These resolutions
might sometimes be transmuted with the assent of the *patres*
into decisions that affected the whole citizen body once they
had been approved in the Assembly of Centuries on the proposal of a magistrate of the whole people. The plebeian tribunes
were protected by an agreed sacrosanctity, which meant that

while they protected the plebeians, they were themselves protected by the support of the plebeian body, which guaranteed their security.[9] The two Orders in the community, patricians and plebeians, might seem to divide it, but it could be maintained that they held it together by a characteristic give and take, effective to secure the *dignitas* of the patricians and at the same time the *libertas* of the common people.

Thus the acceptance of the right of the patricians to supply the executive and to enjoy the *imperium,* and to form at least the very great majority of the Senate, was balanced by the admission of the right of the plebeians to be protected by men of their own choosing from arbitrary wrong. This protection was extended about the middle of the fifth century by the formulation of a code of law, called the Twelve Tables, which, however conservative in character and limited in scope, did at least make known and constant the bases of judgment.

But this code sought to establish or to maintain a prohibition of intermarriage between patricians and non-patricians, a prohibition which would perpetuate the social division of the two Orders in the community. This prohibition was within a few years revoked, and patrician and plebeian gentry, if they could not become brothers, could at least become brothers-in-law. But the fusion of the patrician aristocracy and the plebeian gentry was slow to come about, and the Roman People continued to be governed by a chief executive that was almost wholly patrician. But otherwise the plebeians could protect their liberty and such rights as they possessed, and patrician control over acts of plebeian meetings or assemblies in which plebeians were the majority was gradually relaxed.

Meanwhile there was a long period which is usually compendiously described as the Struggle of the Orders, the patricians struggling to maintain privileges, the plebeians struggling to acquire them. While admitting that something of the kind was inevitable, I would adhere to the view that the phrase "the Struggle of the Orders" implies more than the truth. It is not out of place, in order to see Roman ideas and practice in a just perspective, to consider briefly the three main sources of our knowledge of the internal history of the Early Republic. The first, the most familiar, source is to be found in the literary tradition that has survived, above all, in the pages of Livy. When that admirable and sincere man of letters wrote in the reign of Augustus, the dominant form of the literary tradition was that presented by a group of annalists or historians who belonged to the earlier part of the first century B.C. These writers had dramatized the story that had come to them from their predecessors by attributing to the Romans of the early Republic the political controversies of their own time.[10] Granted that their main purpose was to produce a literary effect, we may suspect (what the evidence does not exist to prove) that they also sought to give a respectable antiquity to the political techniques of the later *Populares*. The strong political colouring found in Livy and apparent in other writers of his day, as Dionysius of Halicarnassus, agrees with what is known of the point of view of those particular later annalists and historians to whom Livy not infrequently refers. Their activity has been well described by an eminently discerning Italian scholar as a process of romance-making rather than of reconstruction.[11] If this be true, as I believe it to be, we must refuse to accept, or at least regard with the utmost scepticism, those elements in the literary tradition which appear to spring from this process of political romance.

The second source is to be found in the Fasti, that is, the lists of magistrates which claim to go back to the beginning of the Republic. These lists, for the first half century or so of the

Republic, do not appear to be so securely based on contemporary records, written or preserved by tradition, as to deny the possibility that they are, in part, conjecture or fabrication. Thereafter, however, the Fasti become trustworthy apart from some few names which are reasonably suspected as due to much the same kind of process as affected the literary tradition. Granted this, the Fasti provide a means of reaching the truth more promising, so far as it goes, than the literary tradition.

The third source is what can be deduced from well-attested Roman institutions of a later period. The Romans (even though denied the opportunity of perusing the pages of Mommsen's *Staatsrecht*) studied their own institutions and made some shrewd deductions which are of real value. This is the more so if, as we may reasonably assume, the Romans thought about their institutions when they studied them in much the same way as they had thought about them when they created them. The institutions of other Italian communities may also be of value, but the evidence for them is not abundant, and their institutions are more often modelled on Rome than themselves models which Rome followed.[12] Some eminent scholars are inclined also to use the early political institutions of Greek city-states as a guide to the probable course of Roman political development. But this may prove misleading, for where we do know for certain what the Greeks and the Romans did in such matters, they seem to see things very differently. Finally it has been urged by some that as Nature, we are told, does not proceed *per saltum*, so neither did Roman institutions.[13] This doubtless would imply that each constitutional act must follow logically or naturally from some predecessor. I am told by those who know more about Nature than I do that nowadays she is not so consequent as all that, and it may be the Roman Republic was not so consequent either. Its natural conservatism

did not preclude developments which do not appear to follow
logically from its former practice. Having said as much as this,
I must endeavour to be consistent with my view of the evidence
and may be forgiven if I give or assume a cautious, rather
prosaic, view of the development of the Early Republic and
its apparent rationale, which will be apparent if we trace the
history of the chief executive of the State over the eighty years
or so that followed the promulgation of the Twelve Tables in
the middle of the fifth century.[14]

What we would have expected if a Struggle of the Orders
were the main content of Republican history is that, gradually
but steadily, plebeians would succeed in becoming members of
the pairs of consuls. What in fact happened, as is shown by the
Fasti, was that for nearly half a century the Republic had, in
some years but not in others, three or four magistrates called
military tribunes with consular power instead of a pair of
consuls. Then for a period of about the same length, the dual
consulship almost disappears: in its place the Fasti present a
series of sets of no fewer than six of these military tribunes with
consular power. The literary tradition seeks to explain these
phenomena as due to an attempt to provide non-patricians with
opportunities of securing high office without giving them access
to the consulship.[15] But this explanation is refuted by the fact
that non-patricians are very rarely elected, and political expedi-
ents do not long survive repeated failures to secure their ends.
An alternative explanation[16] that in the first of these periods
Rome needed more generals or administrative officers in one
year than another cannot be the whole story. For the choice
between two consuls and one of these more numerous colleges
of magistrates was bound to be taken too early to suit the
military needs of the following campaigning season, and, on
the other hand, the choice was too irregular to suit administra-

tive needs which could hardly vary from year to year. During the second period the groups of six magistrates are so very often wholly patrician in membership that they do not reveal a progressively increasing admission of plebeians to high office, and though this period was in general a period of military stress it is hard to understand so great a permanent increase in the number of chief magistrates. And it seems a paradox that the Republic then returned to the constant appointment of pairs of consuls in which plebeian members are usually found. The literary tradition and the evidence of the Fasti do not in fact fit well together, the notion that institutions developed with a logical continuity will not fit the facts, and the constitutional experience of other city-states does not afford any clear parallel[17] which might help to provide an explanation for the facts offered by the Fasti which must, in the main, be accepted as historical. It is difficult to escape the conclusion that what is traditionally called the Struggle of the Orders reflects, not so much a deep-seated continuing sickness in the State as the growing-pains of the body politic, not so much a cleavage of sentiment as the working out of a more lasting unity of the Roman People.

After this long period of experiment to meet the needs of the State, there followed a decade of conflict between the ambitions of the plebeian gentry together with the economic needs of the commons on the one hand and the great predominance of patrician government on the other. This conflict ended in an agreement between patricians and plebeians which, apart from a few early exceptions, became the rule that governed the election of the chief magistrate. There was a final return to the dual magistracy of the consulship, but with the proviso that became absolute that one of the two consulships should be reserved for a plebeian.[18] Granted that the relatively small patrician aristocracy had suffered losses in war and some natural decline in numbers, it was a striking act of patriotic self-abnegation to give up what had been not far from a monopoly of high office. And, more important still, it reflects the fact that a new patrician-plebeian nobility was taking the place of the old patrician aristocracy.

Thus the social equalization of patrician and plebeian notables was translated into a sharing of political power, even if for some purposes the patricians in the Senate retained prerogatives of their own. A nobility, conferred on members of leading families by holding office, made aristocracy secure by broadening its basis. The economic troubles of the commons were gradually reduced and almost removed by wise legislation, and by the founding of colonies, which at once strengthened Roman power and made land available for settlement.

In the two generations of warfare and diplomacy that followed this agreement about the consulship, Rome came to control almost all Central Italy. Conflicts with her old allies the Latins and Hernici were turned to good purpose by statesman-like generosity in moments of victory, until Rome became the head of an Italian federation which put at her disposal most of the manpower of peninsular Italy. Thus the united strength of the Republic was enhanced by this co-operation of Rome and many of her neighbours.

The last question in dispute between the two Orders, the patricians and plebeians, the general validity of the legislation in the *Concilium* of the plebeians on the proposal of tribunes, was solved by the unfettered acceptance of plebeian resolutions as binding upon patricians and plebeians alike.[19] The Senate became the representative body of the new nobility as it had once been the representative body of the old patrician aristocracy.

The Senate was, it is to be remembered, an advisory body, not either legislative or executive in its own right. When it suggested to magistrates that they should do this or that, it added the proviso "if it seemed good to them to do so". But as it comprised all or almost all of those who had held high office, it embodied the administrative experience of the ruling class, and for experience the Romans always had a high respect. Roman magistrates did not flinch from responsibility, but they normally believed that in a number of counsellors there is wisdom. And the problems of the young Republic tended to be recurrent problems. That shrewd observer, George Savile, Marquess of Halifax, declared that to be a good prophet you needed a good memory, and the Romans in making policy drew largely on the form of memory which is experience.

It was admitted that when the whole People met to legislate, their assent was a command, their refusal to assent a prohibition. But it was not for the People but for the magistrates, usually advised by the Senate, to decide the subject on which their sovereign voice should be heard. When the People elected a magistrate it was from among names put before them by a presiding officer of state, and when a magistrate entered office his commission could not be revoked. And what was true of the magistrates of the whole People was roughly true of the officers of the plebeians.

As the magistrates were apt to have regard to the corporate experience of the Senate, so the People in the early Republic tended to have regard to the experience of the magistrates and to their record of success especially in war. Thus in periods of military stress the early Republic had almost always turned to members of the patrician clans who had proved themselves as generals, men who would work well with colleagues of their own stamp. As military crises were met by resolute unity, so economic or political crises were at least mitigated by recourse to occasional compromise.

The acceptance of the right of plebeians to occupy at least one of the two chief regular offices of the State was followed by their admission to one after another of the other magistracies, the dictatorship, the office of praetor, of censor and so on. The ambitions of the plebeian gentry were gradually satisfied. The acceptance, early in the third century, of resolutions of the plebeian *Concilium* on the initiative of the tribunes as binding on the whole People and not subject to revision by the *patres* marks the end of the first phase of tribunician progress.

It is now in place to say something more about that institution and the ideas that it embodied.

On the earliest beginnings of the plebeian tribunate the ancient evidence is conflicting, but it seems clear that by the middle of the fifth century the *Concilium* of the plebeians elected ten tribunes each year with the possibility of re-election. Their activity was limited to the city and did not challenge the military *imperium* of the consuls in the sphere described as *militiae,* the field of war.[20] But they stood for all the plebeians and not those alone who actually resided in the city. Their claim to protect plebeians may reflect their primary purpose and was at first their normal activity. As has been said, they stood for *libertas* of the small man[21] and in this they had the support of all such, and their personal immunity was assured by the fact that they were protected by those they protected. The plebeians were needed for the defence of the community, and the possibility that the tribunes might lead a kind of military strike of plebeians had to be taken into account. They were probably not so political in their activities as the literary tradition would suggest. Yet in the plebeian body there were not only small men who needed protection from misusage but substantial gentry whose ambitions were denied by any patrician monopoly of office. It is at least probable that most of the tribunes were such men, who sought to rise from *libertas* to *dignitas*, and in the end achieved their purpose. As the Senate influenced the magistrates by their *auctoritas*, so the tribunes became able to influence magistrates and the Senate alike by a declaration that they and their plebeian clients would resist magisterial acts which impinged upon what they regarded as their rights. They thus restricted the initiative of magistrates. This intervention, called *intercessio*, could be regarded as an anticipation and generalization of their right of help to individuals, but it came to mean more than that. It came to mean that obstruction in matters that did not directly concern only the plebeians was recognized, at least by custom, as an instrument of internal politics.

The sacrosanctity of the tribunes passed from defence to attack when the claim was asserted to use force against a magistrate who crossed their will. Finally the initiative of the tribunes in proposing resolutions in the *Concilium* of the plebeians was free, even if the resolutions were not yet binding upon the whole of the Roman People. And when at last they were admitted to be binding, the will of the plebeians in legislation was potentially an overriding power in the State. There was the possibility of rule by the People, and yet the Roman community continued almost all the time to be aristocratically governed. The new nobility of office, which embraced both patricians and plebeians, and the Senate that represented that nobility, remained the trusted instruments of day-to-day government, and the day-to-day creators of policy, for that was and continued to be the tradition of Rome. And though the tribunes, whose activity was restricted to the precincts of the city, might, one would think, use their power to promote urban interests, Rome remained in this period more a peasant community than anything else. And this was, in large measure, due to the constitution of the Roman assemblies in legislation and in election.[22]

The crisis that led to the recognition of the resolutions of the plebeians as binding on the whole community was probably economic rather than political in origin.[23] The recognition itself may have reflected also the fact that legislation in a meeting voting by tribes, as was true of the *Concilium* of the plebeians and later of an Assembly of the whole People, was simpler and more expeditious than the complicated procedure of the Assembly of Centuries. The sectional character of the meetings of the Plebs was passing away, and in all probability patricians were no longer excluded from these meetings, so it was near enough true to say that the voice of the whole Roman People prevailed in these meetings. The characteristic peasant character of the Roman People was preserved by the fact that the existing territorial division of the citizen body into tribes based upon residence gave a great predominance to those who lived in the countryside as against the growing non-agrarian population of the city itself, for this was limited to members of only four tribes out of a number that grew until it reached thirty-five in all. As the voting was in terms of tribes, the comparatively thinly populated areas of the rustic tribes were at an advantage. Granted that, with all public meetings held in Rome, the urban dwellers were on the spot, whereas peasants might have to make a journey to attend, those peasants who did come counted, each of them, for far more than freedmen or craftsmen who formed the majority of the urban tribesmen. The clients of the nobility who lived in the countryside could be induced to attend by loyalty to their noble patrons, so that the general temper of a tribal Assembly was still apt to be decided by the wishes of the nobility. The election of the higher magistrates of the whole people remained with the Assembly of Centuries, which was so organized that the will of the upper classes was almost certain to prevail.

To return to the development of Roman power: the diplomacy and strategy of Rome had for decades been guided by a wise, cautious but determined group of nobles, some patrician, some plebeian, backed by the experience of the Senate which had known when moderation, generosity, best served the interests of the Republic. As Rome became dominant in Central Italy, the Roman community had enlarged its borders and, still more, bound her neighbours to herself by a gradation of privileges and alliances which displayed a statesmanship hitherto unknown in the ancient world. But while we may suppose that the majority of the governing class were content with a policy of rest and be thankful, there arose men who promoted a more active foreign policy and were ready to invoke as tribunes, or by way of tribunes, the newly won legislative power of the People to advance their policy.

Within a very few years the Romans were committed to the defence of the Greek city of Thurii against her Lucanian neighbours by the act of a tribune invoking the powers of the plebeian *Concilium*. It is probable that behind this lay the influence of two plebeian notables, Fabricius and Manius Curius, who, in fact, conducted the operations that followed. If this be so, it was an early instance of that co-operation between generals and tribunes which was to play a great part in the politics of the last half century of the Republic. With them was also associated an Appius Claudius of that headstrong family which had no conventional prejudices and no care for the conservative policies of its fellow senators. A Roman

garrison in Thurii was an intrusion into the sphere of influence
of Tarentum, which traditionally sought to preserve the fish-
ing in the troubled waters of South Italy, and its expulsion was
one cause of the war with Pyrrhus. Now and again also, after
the First Punic War, the scanty records of that period show a
restless activity and a readiness to *brusquer* neighbouring
powers, even the formidable monarchy of Macedon just before
the outbreak of the Hannibalic War.

And finally, this tendency was most strikingly exemplified
when a tribune, C. Flaminius, carried a proposal to divide
among citizen settlers a tract of land taken from the Gauls of
Northern Italy.[24] This proposal could be defended on economic
and also on military grounds, but it had its dangers and was
pressed through against strong opposition in the Senate. It led
to a hard-fought war with the Gauls, and it was arguable that
it was more bold than wise, despite its success. It challenged the
Senate's direction of foreign policy and revealed a secret of
empire: that this policy could be made outside the Senate.
It was long remembered and condemned in conservative
circles as a dangerous precedent.

By the time of these events a change had been made in the
voting organization of the Assembly of the Centuries.[25] The
character of this change is, and is likely to remain, in dispute,
but in some way the Centuries were linked with the local tribes,
which had now reached the number of thirty-five. Whatever
view is taken of the character and purpose of this change, its
effect would be to give a majority to substantial peasants. The
advantage given to the country voters by the tribal system
would limit the effect of the growth in numbers of the members of the four city tribes, and, in so far would help to maintain the agrarian character of the community. On the other
hand it would restrict the political effect of the clients of the

great aristocratic families so far as these belonged to the city tribes. It has been observed that within the two decades in which this reform of the Centuriate Assembly must fall, nine new families figure in the list of consuls, which implies some widening of the new nobility of office and some diminution of the influence of the older *gentes*, patrician and plebeian alike.

The scanty evidence for the internal political events of these years does not enable us to detect with any certainty what would be their natural effect on constitutional development. The admitted right of the commons to take decisions on some matters and the lack of any legal bar to their taking decisions on others might mean that the Republic was on the way to develop into an agrarian democracy. In the confidence of power, the Roman People might have taken its own way and found leaders able to make its will prevail. And then there intervened, in this moment of apparent suspense, a military crisis of great range and lasting effect.

III

THE AUTHORITY
OF THE SENATE

As was said at the end of the last chapter, there was the possibility, just before the Hannibalic War, of Rome becoming a democracy in the sense that the plebeian *Concilium* with its unfettered power of legislation might be used by popular leaders to assert its will and theirs. It would still be a peasant democracy, but a democracy none the less. The Republic would not any longer be an aristocracy. Now, in general, it seems that communities are best served by forms of government which match their instinctive likes and dislikes. If this be so, it would be best for the Republic not to substitute democracy for aristocracy, which for so long had been a stabilizing element in the constitution. For *au fond* the Romans liked to be governed by an aristocracy. When I say *au fond* I am reminded of a china figure of a seated mandarin that stood upon my nursery mantelpiece. I rejoiced to tip it this way and that, and to see it settle back into its former demure position. This was because it had *au fond* a stabilizing element, and what lead was to my mandarin, an instinct for aristocracy was to the Roman Republic of this time. And the form in which the aristocracy resumed its unchallenged reign was the assertion and acceptance of the authority of the Senate, which is the topic of this chapter. And the main reason why this happened when it did was that Rome's greatest enemy, Hannibal, unwittingly did

her the service of making the authority of the Senate the necessary and natural expression of the continuing tradition of the
Republic. It was not just that Rome found herself at war—
that had happened often enough before—but in a war which
combined danger, duration and comp lexity in a very high
degree. Defeat followed defeat: at the outset C. Flaminius himself perished in a great disaster at Lake Trasimene. An attempt
to repair this by an offensive in overwhelming force ended in
a yet greater defeat at Cannae. There was a reaction towards
trust in generals from the old aristocratic families, and when
after years of war, victory came, it had been achieved, above
all, by the tenacious unity of the Roman People. It proved, too,
that the statesmen who had built up the great alliance of
Italian communities under Roman leadership were justified by
its over-all loyalty to the Republic. Hannibal's hopes were
refuted in the end, and his most lasting achievement was,
ironically enough, to confirm the power of Rome in Italy and
to induce a long period of stability in its constitution. For the
course and character of the war was such as to establish the
authority of the Senate.

The Hannibalic War, indeed, involved operations in Spain
as well as in Italy; it spread to Sicily and across the Adriatic and
ended in Africa itself. For a war on this scale and of this range,
the annual magistrates could not provide enough generals of
approved skill. The dual consulship was now too deeply rooted
to be abandoned, and direct iteration of office had become rare.
The Republic had indeed for many years past adopted the
expedient of employing magistrates after the expiry of their
year of office by *prorogatio*.[1] The use of this procedure had
become a matter for the judgment of the Senate, and now its
frequent use extended not only the Senate's patronage but its
prestige. Furthermore, the distribution of forces between

commanders in the several theatres of war was bound to fall
to the Senate, which thus provided for an over-all strategy and
balance of effort. Then the supplying of armies required a continuing control of finance in close contact with the military
establishment, and this fell to the Senate co-operating with the
censors, or with the consuls in periods when the censors were
not active. Then when Hannibal and the Carthaginian Government strove, not without success, to raise up a coalition against
Rome, there was need to counter their diplomacy, and this
required a steady policy which the Senate, with its experience
in negotiating with Italian communities during the previous
century, was well fitted to initiate and to guide.[2] Thus foreign
policy became more and more the peculiar care of the Senate.

A rivalry of military policies tinged with a rivalry of
personalities was bound to emerge now and then as the war
went on. The wary and strongheaded Fabius, for example,
might cling to the defensive strategy to which he has given his
name. He was not the first, or the last, general to believe that
what was good enough for him was good enough for
his country. By contrast Scipio, a far greater soldier, believed
that victory was to be found, first by way of Spain and then in
Africa itself. In the end, Scipio prevailed, but it needed the
Senate to arbitrate or conciliate these differences of opinion.
And, finally, the fact that the war went on for more than sixteen years made the Senate's direction of it seem the normal
thing; its steadiness when things went badly, its leadership both
of Rome and of Rome's allies in Italy, the ultimate success of
the generals it trusted, made its ascendancy seem desirable,
indeed desirable to the point of inevitability.

It is instructive to observe that while this was happening,
there was hardly any *formal* change in the structure of the
Roman constitution.[3] No new law changed the rights of the

People or of the plebeians in legislation or in election. Nor did any new law assign to the Senate more powers than it had possessed. No new law conferred on it the command that was *imperium* nor the powers and functions that added up to what the Romans called *potestas*. What happened, and happened without statutory expression, was a great increase of something the Senate already possessed—viz. authority, *auctoritas,* which was a mixture of prestige and initiative. For most of the eighty years that lay between the first victories of Hannibal and the tribunate of Tiberius Gracchus, the part of *auctoritas* that results from prestige continued, and the part of it that results in initiative was enhanced. And the Senate, by custom and for good practical reasons, looked after many things and really settled them. It has been said that what is everybody's business is nobody's business. It may also be said that in well-conducted societies what is nobody's business becomes somebody's business, and in Rome at this time the "somebody" was apt to be the Senate.

Thus the position of the Senate was, in large measure, based on practical utility and necessity.[4] In terms of directly executive officers the Republic was undermanned: the executive itself did not have to assist it a permanent and substantial professional bureaucracy such as the Hellenistic monarchies had possessed.[5] The continuing experience which is offered by a professional bureaucracy was in part supplied by the fact that the Senate contained many men who had had a practical experience as magistrates of almost any administrative problem that arose. One of the main reasons, indeed, for the success of Rome's foreign policy was that it was made by men who knew what carrying out policy meant. So far as such problems were recurrent, as most of them were, the Senate contained within its ranks, if not men who knew all the answers, enough men who knew some of the answers. Thus the Senate, which met diligently and very often, could be entrusted with what were accepted as decisions on many matters which the executive magistrates had not the time or perhaps the knowledge and experience to settle. To such matters it applied its collective mind. As the magistrates were expected to take decisions in accordance with their conscience and the interests of the State, so was the Senate, and the expectation was on the whole not misplaced. And in general it is true that the greater the trust, the greater the sense of responsibility. It is at this point that the idea of *fides*, which has already been described, comes into its own.

There is another thing to be considered. In order to give to enough men the chance of preserving and advancing their *dignitas* by holding high office, the normal tenure of almost all such posts was limited to a year and re-election was rare. The practice of prorogation, which kept some men effectively in office for more than a year, was a very useful expedient, but it was mainly effective in external affairs and that not at the highest level. Throughout most of the second century Rome had to use too many generals to ensure a high degree of generalship in the field and used too many governors to ensure a high standard of government in the provinces. The lack of first-rate commanders was not fully compensated by the training, discipline and morale of the troops, which, indeed, seem to have declined during the period. This weakness was slightly relieved by the Senate's direction of major strategy, and its judgment of generals when special capacities were needed in serious wars. And the foreign policy for which the Senate was mainly responsible helped by adding to the legions and Italian allies other troops of military value. The government of the provinces was not easy to control from Rome, but something was done by the Senate, though not enough. All in all, the ascendancy of the Senate mitigated the defects of an order of things in which too many magistrates tried to distinguish themselves beyond their capacity or to solve administrative problems beyond their knowledge.

Granted all this, we must reach the general conclusion that at Rome in these years policy was made within the Senate, even if it was executed by the magistrates, and even if generals and governors had much freedom in conducting operations and government in provinces and theatres of war. This does not, however, mean that the Senate was a body of men who all thought the same on public questions, or that the Senate's policy in one year need be the Senate's policy in the next. There was no question of the Senate being dominated year after year by a majority pledged to a constant attitude to all public questions based upon unvarying principles and long-range programmes. It was true that the Senate consisted almost entirely of men of the same social class, but within its ranks there was room for a wide diversity of opinion; there were present in it groups of senators who supported this or that opinion and sought to enable members of the group to make their influence prevail. And it did, indeed, still matter who were the men whom the People elected to high office, and the Senate as a body could not control the elections of the great magistrates by the People, nor the choice of the tribunes by the plebeians.

The careful study of the opinions of magistrates and influential generals, and of the composition of groups of senators which supported them, has gone far to explain variations of Roman policy and to reveal the rivalries and ambitions of members of the nobility.[6] But it remains true that the Curia was the clearing house of opinion, and that what was decided there, however it was decided, was, for the time being, the prevailing policy of the State. And in point of fact, the policy made in the Senate, though it was not uniform and need not be self-consistent, tended to reflect the general character of senatorial opinion with at least some unity in diversity.

One primary reason for this was that the Senate formed its policy after a debate in which its senior members were allowed to have the first word. And this, in bodies with a high respect for experience and a high regard for authority, tends to be not only the first word but the last. The magistrates who presided in the Senate had freedom in what they laid before it, but it was not in practice easy to avoid a debate on any matter of serious importance. And it was equally difficult for magistrates to disregard the effect of a vote which was reached after a discussion, in which the authority of the seniors was apt to have more influence than eloquence or dialectic. The fragments of speeches that have survived from this period almost everywhere reveal a forceful and clear statement of opinion which is well fitted to make debate fruitful. It was the rule that the relevant facts on any question were made known to the Senate by the presiding magistrates; and too many other men had a chance of knowing them and the right to mention them for them not to be taken into account. It is almost axiomatic that, whatever the form of government, decisions on policy are made by those "in the know", and the Roman Senate, from the senior consular to the most junior member, had normally the advantage of being "in the know".

Granted all this, it is to be remembered that the Senate had not a *statutory* monopoly of policy making. The consuls still possessed their ancient rights. The Senate had not, *by law*, any veto on their actions: it had no legal power to prevent consuls or praetors from invoking the legislative power of the People meeting in their assemblies of centuries or tribes, and giving effect to the People's command. Equally, and more significantly, the Senate could not legally prevent a tribune proposing a resolution in the meeting of the plebs which, if carried on whatever topic, had direct binding force on the whole State. As will be remembered, the tribune C. Flaminius had, despite the opposition of the Senate, settled the question of occupying the Gallic land in North Italy by the simple *fiat* of the plebeian *Concilium*.[7] What was there to prevent this happening again and again?

The short answer is that the Senate had absorbed the tribunate. And the short answer to the question why this had happened is that the tribunes had lost, as it were, their old constituency. Most at least of the plebeian gentry whose claims tribunes had promoted were now members of the nobility of office. They had no need of tribunes, for their ambitions were satisfied. The plebeian commons did not have to fear general oppression from the magistrates or the rich. It should be remembered that there were ten tribunes all continuously resident in the city, and there could hardly be enough grievances to keep them all employed. There was no plebeian opposition for the tribunes to lead, and so they had joined the government, which could find a use for them.[8]

They had gained admission to the debates of the Senate and so were "in the know"; they were apt to be young men hoping for advancement in office, and so were inclined to be guided by the kind of men they hoped to become; and they could propose measures in the *Concilium* of the plebeians with its simple and expeditious procedure, and that at the suggestion of magistrates. As the Senate could request magistrates to propose measures in the Assemblies of the whole People, so they could ask magistrates to induce tribunes to do that very thing in the *Concilium Plebis*. Of the known plebiscites passed in the eighty years we are considering, that is, between the beginning of the Hannibalic War and the Gracchi, only four were carried without or against the will of the Senate.[9] These four were very probably on the prompting of the elder and of the younger Scipio who both had a strong predilection for getting their way in what seemed to them a good cause. More than that, magistrates who showed an inclination to disregard the opinion of the Senate might be subjected to tribunician obstruction or the effect of tribunician legislation. Thus the tribunes, the very people who had challenged the authority of the Senate in the past, became, for a time, one of its most effective instruments. But it is to be remembered that this was by virtue of powers which could equally well be asserted against the Senate by men who were ready to break with the convention on which its predominance really rested.

At this point it is proper to refer to a judgment of the Roman constitution made by Polybius, an experienced Greek statesman and soldier, who had been deported to Rome in the middle years of the second century. He wrote a history of high merit, in which he gave especial attention to the reasons why Rome had become the most powerful state in the Mediterranean world. As a practical soldier he discerned and described the advantages of the military organization of the Republic; as a practical diplomat, he discussed the advantages of Roman foreign policy. But more was needed to complete the picture. The main secret of Roman greatness, he believed, was to be found in its political institutions. In the Hellenistic world states were, roughly speaking, monarchies, aristocracies or democracies, and now, in terms of power, none of them could match Rome. Applying to this problem the results of Greek political speculation, Polybius declared that the main cause of Rome's success during the fifty years that followed the beginning of the Hannibalic War was that the Republic had been a harmonious blending of the three types of government—monarchy, aristocracy and democracy.[10]

In his *Sixth Book* he maintains and illustrates this doctrine. We are not concerned with the higher criticism of Polybius' history at this point or with his belief in an inevitable process of change in the life of states. What matters here is that he finds in the tribunes the main evidence for the democratic element, in the great magistrates the main evidence for the monarchical element, in the Senate the manifestation of the aristocratic element. These elements interact on each other; the constitution is what Greek philosophers called a mixed, or composite, constitution, and herein lies the secret of its effectiveness. But it is desirable to remember that this conclusion may be itself mixed or composite. It may combine practical observation, the tradition of Roman history as it then was, and philosophical speculation, in which Polybius was, after all, an amateur. It would, indeed, be strange if all of it has an equal claim to be accepted as valid.

What Polybius says about the power of the tribunes as evidence that there was a democratic element in the Roman constitution was denied by realities in the very period which he was setting out to describe.[11] This period is the half century between c. 216 and 168 B.C. and within this period there was time enough for changes and developments which Polybius fails to take into account. And it was just far enough removed from the time at which he was writing for his historical perspective to be faulty.

We may now turn to the magistrates of the whole people, especially the consuls. The powers and high dignity of the magistrates are adduced by Polybius as evidence of a monarchical element in the Roman State.[12] But whatever they were, the magistrates were not in reality monarchical in the sense of monarchy as it existed in the kingdoms of the day or in Rome before the establishment of the Republic. The *imperium* where it was exercised had the old validity, the dignity of the consuls was unimpaired, but the magistrates were annual, and immediate re-election was ruled out first by practice and then by law. When Cicero speaks of the *imperium* of the consuls being "regal" he adds the words "albeit annual".[13] The Spartan kingship was shared by two kings, but then these kings were kings for life. When the consuls were in Rome they would not disregard the authority of the Senate; when they led armies in the field they led them unhampered, but they were usually the agents of an agreed policy not of their own making, with forces assigned to them by the Senate. When they negotiated with foreign powers, their *acta* were generally subject to senatorial confirmation. When they won victories, it was the Senate that decided whether they should receive the crowning honour of a triumph.[14] A monarch so responsible to an august body which was described as an assembly of kings[15] was not a monarch at all. The dictatorship, which had a monarchical character for the period of its tenure, was now a thing of the past, though it was to know a survival in the future.

Of all this Polybius can hardly have been unaware. But he sacrifices too much reality in order to define the Roman constitution in terms of Greek philosophic speculation. There was a democratic element, but it was latent. There was a strong executive, but it was the agent of policies which were not of its own unfettered making. The day-to-day reality in the Roman State was the authority of the nobility vested in its vehicle the Senate, indirectly derived from the choice of the Roman People, but not under its day-to-day control. What the Rome of the Middle Republic was, was an aristocracy guiding the state by a corporate authority—*auctoritas* had come into its own.

It may be significant that this very word *auctoritas* is a technical term in the practice of the Senate. It was possible for the Senate to be prevented from converting its opinion into a decision by the intervention—the *intercessio*—of a tribune. But this intervention was only permitted after the debate and after the expression of opinion had been generalized in a vote.[16] This vote was preserved and placed on record, and the word used of it was *auctoritas*, which, as I have said, contained the idea of initiative, and what the Senate thought was therefore not thought in vain. But powerful as the authority of the Senate was, it would persist while it justified its existence but not longer, for it was at the mercy of its own shortcomings and, in the last analysis, it needed the steady acceptance by the Roman People of its right to persist. Such was the *auctoritas* of the Senate, something that did not rest upon statute but on the cumulative influence of a number of families that had provided the highest magistrates by the choice of the Roman People, and which between them constituted those called *nobiles*. By now the nobles had become exclusive, for it had become very rare for anyone outside these families to be elected to high office. And round these *nobiles* gathered the other members of the senatorial Order whose families, though they provided magistrates, had not reached the highest offices of State.

Generations before, the patricians had been the nobility, but there had been added to them plebeian families who attained high office and had become, in effect, their partners in the ruling aristocracy, until the two elements were effectively fused together in one single aristocratic body. It may seem strange that this process of expansion did not continue. There was an increasing class of well-to-do Romans who might, one would expect, enjoy a like promotion if their ambition lay that way. And yet this extension of the senatorial Order did not occur. One part of the reason for this is reflected in a law passed on the eve of the Second Punic War which denied to the senatorial Order investment in seagoing undertakings by prohibiting their ownership of vessels of any size.[17] Senators, so it seems, continued to comprise the great landowners and left to those outside their ranks the other means of prosperity, by investment in commerce and by finance.[18] While senators who lived by their land, and at times profited from the spoils of war if they held high command, devoted themselves to the direction of the government, there arose a second economic Order of rich men—the *equites,* who satisfied their energies in these other ways. In leaving to them this profitable sphere of activity, the senatorial aristocracy retained for itself the satisfaction of its *dignitas* in office and the control of high matters of State. Among the *equites* there was bound to grow up an *esprit de corps,* but for its rapid and significant growth it lacked a representative body like the Senate to give it leadership and a sense of direction. This did not mean that this Second Estate had no interest in the results of senatorial policy. Its members served the State for financial reward by undertaking the provision of State services such as the making of roads, the building of public works, the supplying of fleets and armies, and the contracting for payment in advance of provincial taxes or revenues. The needs of the State were their opportunity, as was the expansion of Roman power overseas. But they accepted the fact that war and foreign policy rested with the senatorial Order which provided the direct agents for both.

It can be argued that, on balance, the separation of the governing senatorial Order from the Second Estate, the financial and commercially minded Order of the *equites,* was a good thing and not a bad. In most communities it has often been observed that government is best conducted when those entrusted with it are not too permeated by what may be called big business. In Great Britain, for instance, members of the Government of the day are not permitted to have financial commitments which might deflect their judgment. And though this separation between senators and *equites* could be, in a measure, evaded, a mixture of social prejudice and traditional responsibility kept the two Orders each in its own place.

In economic policy in Italy it was, however, a weakness of the senatorial regime that it became too much concerned with the interests of the great landowners of its own class. For the revenues derived from land were the chief means whereby the senators met the heavy expenditure on themselves and others which their rank demanded of them. The more land monopolized their interests, the more they tended to monopolize land. If they did their duty as they saw it, their sight was short and dim. They ceased to be active in promoting the agrarian interests of the whole Roman People.

It is true that in the generation that followed the end of the Hannibalic War the Roman Government did much for the rehabilitation of Roman and Italian farming and to repair the effect of devastation. Colonies of citizens and Latin colonies and individual settlements on public land made good use of territory that came under Roman state control. But to all appearances, the temptations offered by the availability of slave labour in the hands of great landowners prevailed over the older liberality that had been of benefit to some Italians and very many Romans. The maintenance and advancement of power overseas imposed on the Roman peasants and the Italian allies of the Republic military burdens which bore hardly upon both. The concentration of policy in the Senate, its preoccupa-

tion with foreign affairs, and its lack of economic insight meant
that serious domestic problems were in part unrealized in part
neglected. Thus in this field there became visible shortcomings
which undermined the authority of the Senate. A sense of
security born of success induced inertia, and the virtues born
of danger became outmoded.[19] Senatorial complacency became
impatient of criticism by its own kind and there was no widespread public opinion to reveal discontent at home, and yet
the discontent was there, and in this field the authority of the
Senate was slowly undermined. On the other hand, in external
affairs, there was much success, more perhaps than senatorial
policy deserved.

The motives of Roman foreign policy in this period and the
influence upon it of great personages with their followers fall
outside the scope of this inquiry. They affect the stages of the
advance of Roman power rather than its over-all effect. For
it is, in general, true that shifts of policy, diplomatic errors
and occasionally military reverses did not impair the ascendancy
of the Senate in this field. The two great military assets of the
Republic, its great manpower in Roman and Italian troops and,
though to a lesser degree, its shrewd capacity for enlisting the
forces of foreign allies against foreign enemies, made ultimate
success certain. There was room for more generosity and wisdom and less self-deception. Rome sometimes unwittingly
served interests other than her own, or was malignant without sufficient cause, but in the long run her material power
became greater and her prestige extended even beyond her
power.

In this process may be discerned a development of Roman
statecraft. The strong system of alliances in Italy built up before
the Hannibalic War had rested on a gradation of privilege
together with respect for the autonomy of the allies, subject to

a provision of military assistance.[20] It stood for the defence of Italy under Roman leadership. The aristocracy of the Republic was, it may be assumed, on good terms with the aristocracies of the Italian communities. This general system of alliances familiar to the Romans was not abandoned when Rome entered the world of the Hellenistic states, though the Senate also made use of their more flexible diplomatic methods. City-states, alone or in federation, were regarded as natural allies so long as they were prepared to pursue policies that suited Roman interests. Kings and princes could count on Roman protection and help if they were dutiful clients: city-states could be mobilized against them if they appeared dangerous. In the Hellenistic world the practice of arbitration was already developed, and this matched Roman legal ideas. Where the Republic's interests were not directly concerned, the Senate encouraged arbitration and so assisted the peaceful settlement of quarrels. In the field the Romans were apt to be harsh and drastic beyond the normal practice of Hellenistic warfare, but the old tradition of moderation in victory was not wholly forgotten. It seemed to outside observers that Rome had notably resisted the temptations of great strength. When at last, in 146 B.C., Rome destroyed both Corinth and Carthage, the whole Mediterranean world was profoundly shocked.[21] It seemed, as indeed it was, a sudden lapse from the general moderation of Roman policy, a denial of ideals which were beginning to affect the thinking of the Roman governing class or at least an enlightened group within its ranks.

There are two things to be said about this. The first is that many Romans had come to believe that they were a master race. They believed that they were a chosen people, with peculiar gifts of morale and statecraft that justified their power. This belief was given an ethical content with the help of the Stoic philosopher, Panaetius, who adapted Greek philosophical ethics to the instincts of the Roman governing class. He was not just a flatterer of the great, or merely concerned to provide the top dog with a philosophic collar. He geared together the Stoic idea of moral duty and the old Roman idea of *fides,* which means that you must use your strength fairly and conscientiously and rule with a care for the good of those you govern. To this high duty Rome was called, and this high duty was the legacy of Rome's past, the ancient care to preserve the good will of the gods, which had repaid piety with prosperity. These ideas provided a half-philosophical and half-religious justification of the expansion of Roman power. To this was added in some senatorial circles the salutary fear that security would mean the disintegration of the unity of the State, that ambitions and rivalries would make the Romans their own enemies when they had no other enemies to guard against.[22]

The second thing is this. The virtues of the Romans tended to be community virtues, strong in their setting of community life. Outside the community, when unguarded by a traditional code of action in the sight of one's fellows, these virtues seemed to lose much of their compelling force. It had been a reproach against the Spartans that, while at home they were models of virtue, once they went abroad they governed harshly and governed ill. This became only too often true of the Roman aristocrats: when they left the society of their peers, and went abroad to see that Rome got her way and her revenues, they failed to pack their consciences in their baggage. There was much exploitation and misgovernment of subject communities and it was getting worse. And the Italian allies of Rome who now had to fight not to defend Italy but to spread and maintain Roman power had less than their share of the rewards of victory and more than their share of the losses of defeat.

And so, for all the outward success of the senatorial regime there was much to disquiet enlightened and public-spirited aristocrats, who, like most Roman reformers, believed that better times were to be reached by going backwards. This may not be the best way to progress, and it is dangerous to go backwards too fast. That danger was to be exemplified in the careers of Tiberius Gracchus and his brother Gaius, and in the age of revolution which challenged too vehemently the static convention of senatorial authority.

IV

THE AGE OF REVOLUTION

THE CENTURY that preceded the appearance of the Gracchi had meant the rule of a convention—for that is what it was—the convention being embodied in the ascendancy or authority of the Senate, itself the embodiment of an aristocracy of birth and office in one. The Gracchi challenged this convention through the combination of tribunes and People which remained latent in the constitution. For in form and structure the constitution still was what it had been before the convention began its reign. When Tiberius Gracchus and the group of enlightened nobles that backed him in a reasonable programme of agrarian reform could not get their beneficent way, he called on the People to assert its sovereignty. More than that, he invoked it against a fellow tribune who sought to veto his proposal, and the tribune was deposed by a vote of the plebeians. This deposition asserted, or at least assumed, a doctrine that prevailed in democratic Athens but was alien to the spirit of Roman institutions, viz. the doctrine that the People might depose an elected officer if he did not do what the People wished, or could be persuaded to think they wished, at any moment. He also encroached on the Senate's special field of foreign policy by invoking the plebeian *Concilium* to settle the use of possessions which a client king bequeathed to Rome. Finally, as most of Tiberius' friends deserted him when he came into conflict with the Senate, he seemed too insistent upon his own leadership and sought to continue it by immediate re-election as tribune. For the re-election of tribunes there was ancient precedent, but now that the tribunes had been so nearly assimilated to the normal magistrates, their re-election was against the practice of the day.[1] To appeal to the sovereignty of the People without regard to the limitations of convention came near to a democratic revolution. To fortify the will of an individual by this appeal challenged senatorial authority. What the great Scipio had not claimed it was not for a young Gracchus to claim in despite of the aristocratic convention. The petulant violence that had, a decade earlier, invaded Rome's foreign policy invaded domestic controversy, and Tiberius was killed by aristocratic die-hards. "The champions of the constitution could boast that they had shed the first blood drawn in civil war since the expulsion of the second Tarquin."[2]

The agrarian reform of Gracchus was not annulled, but its application was limited when it came into conflict with senatorial responsibility.[3] And the convention was soon challenged again by Gaius Gracchus, who added to a vendetta for his elder brother's death a greater will to power, a more practical energy and a more moving popular appeal. He was elected tribune, and re-elected once, apparently without serious challenge. For nearly two years he and a small group of his followers carried a number of measures most of which deserve the name of reform. But among them there was one which introduced a new ingredient into Roman politics. To procure a make-weight to the influence of the Senate, the Second Order, that of the *equites,* was summoned to a judicial activity which could have a political, sectional effect more often bad than good.

By a plebiscite passed by a follower of Gracchus[4] the *equites* were given the right to supply the jurors in a special court that received complaints of extortion against senatorial governors in the provinces. What remains of the law shows that prosecution was made easy. But senatorial governors were not the only possible offenders. Provincials might and did suffer from oppression by the agents of *equites,* but against that the law gave no protection. Indeed it contained a subtle threat against senatorial governors who sought to restrict these misdeeds, for if they incurred the ill will of the *equites* they might find them unjust judges, and they were not protected against injustice. In the end, the conviction of a governor of exemplary probity who had dared to protect the provincials of Asia made this privilege of the *equites* a question of high politics.[5] It may be observed that the Roman Republic did not bow to the salutary principle that the judiciary should be independent of the executive and without political bias. Thus the *equites* could harry senators. But it is to be remembered that they had an equal interest in the defence of property at home and might join the senatorial Order in securing it. And though they might, now and then, intervene in matters of policy, they were usually content with senatorial policy if it promoted, or at least did not cross, their economic interests.

There was added a second new ingredient in state affairs, this time more external. As was said in the last chapter, the Italian allies of Rome had good grounds for complaint. And now the old statesmanship that had been liberal in extending political rights, and just and tactful in respecting the internal autonomy of the allies, had been forgotten. Roman magistrates had been high-handed,[6] and the members of the Italian communities were not protected by the rights of Roman citizens. They may well have had their own agrarian troubles possibly enhanced and certainly not relieved by the Roman agrarian reforms. Now and again their hopes of better treatment were raised, only to be disappointed. And when, in the closing stages of his career, Gaius Gracchus proposed a wide extension of the Roman franchise to the Italians, he was faced by the indifference or hostility of the Romans from senators to plebeians. But their hopes, though unfulfilled, were not forgotten. Thus what may be called the Italian Question entered the political scene and had at times a disturbing effect, just as the Irish Question in the second half of the nineteenth century had a disturbing effect on English politics.

Meanwhile it had become clear that Gaius Gracchus with a handful of friends could not in fact manage all the state business. He had been borne up on a wave of popular feeling, but waves will be waves, and he ceased to be borne up. His opponents were skilful, some of his supporters played him false. He made a halfhearted move to violence; the leaders of the Senate made a wholehearted countermove by way of a declaration of martial law, and he perished—and many of his adherents too, not only in the fighting but after an inquisition of very doubtful legality.[7]

After the death of Gaius Gracchus there followed half a generation of reaction, in which the government, perhaps a trifle conscience-stricken, showed some approach to economic statesmanship. A lull in foreign wars eased the military burdens of the Italian allies and so diminished their sense of grievance. But though the convention of senatorial authority continued to exist, it had been shaken. Then, owing to troubles in North Africa, the *equites* fell foul of the cautious policy of the Senate, which sought to avoid imperialistic expansion and seemed incapable of crushing a recalcitrant prince. Once more the People was moved to action. Then, when a serious danger from Northern barbarians proved too much for incompetent generals, a bourgeois commander Marius who had been successful in Africa was re-elected consul year after year to maintain the defence of Italy. In the course of achieving this, Marius, already a military innovator, carried through changes in the Roman military machine. These changes made armies more professional and at the same time more prone to look to their generals for rewards which the home government was not able or willing to provide for them. After more than a decade of sporadic internal disorders the Senate was on the way to reassert itself when a new crisis of great moment occurred.[8] The Italian Question became a question of life and death for the Republic.

With the immediate causes of the outbreak of the war between Rome and the greater part of her Italian allies we are not here concerned. It is enough to say that it might have been averted by the timely offer of the enfranchisement which after a hard-fought campaign was in fact made in order to limit the spread of the rising and then to weaken its impact. Victory was won by yielding the fruits of it to the enemy, and an attempt to impair the concession by restricting its purely political effect fortunately failed. What matters most for our purpose is the effect of the enfranchisement in the field of Roman politics and Italian institutions.

This great enfranchisement brought a variant of Roman institutions to new civic communities throughout Italy, but they gained more in local government than in any integration in the Roman State. Some of their notables were able to make careers at Rome, but very rarely at the highest level. Now and then, the general sentiment of the widespread citizen body was manifested,[9] but though the Roman community now extended over all peninsular Italy, most of it could only have a temporary or slight effect on the government of the State. For most purposes public opinion was still the opinion of the aristocratic governing classes, or, at most, of those citizens who lived in or near Rome—and that was all. In ancient conditions of travel and publication this restriction of range was inevitable, and it was not, and perhaps could not be, mitigated by what we would call representative institutions. Apart from some effect on elections the great enfranchisement of Italy had little direct political significance.

There was one occasional indirect effect. In the armies of Rome hitherto, the citizens in their legions had been only a part; now all the soldiers of Italian birth were citizens. So far as legionaries affected politics, they could add to the fact that they had all fought for the Republic the fact that they all belonged to it. They were loyal to Rome against all comers, but they assumed the right to decide that their general had claims on the State which they were entitled to support by force and that the same was true of themselves.

This, however, did not mean that the Roman legions were a *soldateska* led by military adventurers to whom might was right, nor did it mean that Roman politics proceeded under a constant threat of military force by this or that general and army.[10] On the other hand, it is undeniable that what may be called unmilitary violence, exhibited by gangs of roughs, from the senators who killed Tiberius Gracchus to the excitable mobs of the city streets who followed such men as Clodius or Milo, more and more often mocked law and order. The strong tradition that had dedicated the sacred limits of the city to civilian order had faded away. Rome lacked the strong, politically indifferent police force which in great cities is often the surest safeguard of public liberty. One veteran legion encamped upon the Janiculum, ever ready to march in and clear the streets at the first sign of disorder, would have spared the Republic many troubles. A government that can enforce law and order must be a very bad government not to be better than a government that can not.

The concentration of public affairs in Rome, where the cosmopolitan population was not a fair sample of the Roman People, made things worse. But bad behaviour is news while good behaviour is not, and it is easy to overrate the lasting effects of sporadic public disorder and forget that from end to end of peninsular Italy the country towns managed their affairs in an orderly way, and a thrifty and industrious population preserved its ancient virtues in the domesticity in which Italy surpassed its neighbours. And with all the faults of the upper classes in Rome itself they continued to produce hard-headed and resolute soldiers, eminent jurists, eloquent orators, cultivated amateurs of Greek and Latin letters, with that intellectual virtue that was a great part of what they called *humanitas*.

All this is true, but Roman political ideas and practice had now entered upon a revolutionary phase that lasted through the last half century of the Republic, and I must attempt to suggest just what this meant.

The history of this period made it abundantly plain that the convention of senatorial rule could, at intervals and for limited periods, be broken, till in the end it was almost past repair. How was this politically possible and how, on the other hand, could the convention be defended and restored so far as it was defended and restored? In the United States of America, as in Great Britain, the normal process of politics is to have one set of people with one kind of principles and policies in power for a while, and then to try another set of people with rather different principles and policies. In general, the State proceeds by what may seem to some the irrational method of advancing first the right foot and then the left, but it does, none the less, proceed. Why should not Rome have done the same? Why should there not have been a single progressive or democratic anti-senatorial party with principles and programmes to match? This would strive, now successfully now unsuccessfully, against a reactionary or conservative non-democratic or oligarchical, pro-senatorial party also with principles and programmes to match. You would then get the pleasing symmetry of the government and the opposition— the "ins" and the "outs", with "ins" sometimes going out, the "outs" sometimes coming in, with the two-party system, without which Disraeli said parliamentary government is not possible. It used to be believed, and it is still occasionally affirmed, that Roman politics in the last half-century of the Republic were dominated by the conflict of just two such parties. This belief was partly due to the influence of Mommsen's writings, and partly to the established prestige of the English party system of Whigs and Tories, liberals and conservatives, which was widely admired and imitated in other countries. And the belief was assisted by references in ancient writers to people called *Optimates* and people called *Populares* whom it is tempting to equate with conservatives and progressives, oligarchs and democrats.[11] But in fact the words *populares* and *optimates* are usually not so much used of large bodies of people guided by large principles as of leading political figures and their followers. And these leading figures could be described as *Optimate* or *Popular* roughly according as they worked with and through the Senate or with and through the People, especially the *Concilium* of the plebeians. But this was a matter of means rather than ends.

A Roman group in politics was not a large body of men of all classes pursuing principles or far-reaching long-range policies (such as, for instance, nationalization of means of production and exchange), a body of men to whom control of the government is a means to an end, the end being the carrying through of a consistent programme dictated by principles or theories.[12] A Roman political group in the revolutionary age was normally a small group of nobles and their personal adherents pursuing the interests of themselves or their leaders to advance careers, to enjoy power and profits, or to meet some immediate crisis by this or that means, sometimes beneficent but not always so.

Almost all Romans were loyal to the Republic if it seemed to be in danger, but usually Rome was too powerful to be in danger. For by a series of efforts led by very capable soldiers the Republic in the fifty years before the death of Caesar defended, and indeed advanced, the power of Rome. In the absence of salutary dangers from without, Roman politics were constantly bedevilled by rival ambitions: the political stage was too full of actors, all burning to play a leading role.[13] At times the stage was rendered less populous by civil war and its consequences, but it soon filled up again. By way of contrast, in England, for instance in the seventeenth and eighteenth centuries, a nobleman felt himself quite free to keep out of politics: he could enter the Church and become a Bishop or a Dean; he could serve in an army that "dearly loved a Lord"; he could be a country gentleman, a scholarly recluse or a man of fashion sauntering from his club to his tailor and back again; it was no one's business but his own; thus there was room for those noblemen who *did* go in for politics. But in Rome it was otherwise. Roman nobles of the high aristocracy claimed political eminence as their birthright; non-aristocratic men like Cicero sought to secure it as the recognition of their talents. When the poet Lucretius looked on this scene of contending ambitions, he summed up what he saw in three famous lines:

> The strife of wits, the rivalry of birth,
> Through nights and days to toil beyond their peers
> To scale the heights of wealth and master power.[14]

This contest was at too close quarters, the ambitions too insatiable. Where a man's own personal career was not involved, there were the careers of his friends to be advanced, the careers of his enemies to be retarded. The old live-and-let-live, rule-and-let-rule, of the senatorial period had passed. Constitutional forms, the use of precedents, the religious formalities which touched the state practice, all these were exploited by skilful manoeuvres to win, or to retain, power. The course of justice came to be at the mercy of the bribing of juries[15] or deflected by feuds or by the oratory in which many Romans, and not Cicero alone, excelled. The absence of a police force that would defend the government of the day whatever it was, allowed, as I have said, the occasional violence of gangs of roughs, who, at the best, cancelled out each other's efforts. In the year 88 B.C. Sulla, not without some justification, led an army to take Rome; in 87 his enemies did the like. Then Sulla, after winning a Civil War, re-established the powers of the Senate and reduced the power of the tribunes. But then he retired to private life and left the Senate to maintain itself if it could. His safeguards against the revival of anti-senatorial ambitions were not strong enough, or they were not used firmly enough. And his own career was a constant temptation to others to imitate him. Men learnt to say to themselves, as Cicero[16] puts it, "Sulla could do it; shall I not be able to?" (*Sulla potuit, ego non potero?*).

One danger to the stability of the State or at least to the steadying authority of the Senate lay in military emergencies, and for these Sulla seems to have made no regular provision. He had spent more than half his active career fighting in wars of the first importance; now he behaved as though peace had broken out and would be enduring. For small-scale troubles in provinces or client states the Roman military establishment sufficed to arm the regular governors or magistrates, but the Republic had no standing reserves to meet serious enemies.[17] It was necessary to raise armies quickly, which in turn meant the employment of commanders whose prestige would attract back to the eagles, above all, soldiers who had learned, and not yet forgotten, the intricate techniques of Roman warfare in the legions. This might call for a deviation from the standard practice about office and the tenure of the *imperium*, and so demand exceptional decisions. There might be a war in Italy, and Sulla's arrangement left consuls in Italy without the means to take the field in strength. Even before Sulla died there were military emergencies in Italy and in Spain. During the next generation the military needs of the Republic were great and had to be met. The authority and resource of the Senate did not suffice to preserve for it the monopoly of military policy. The Roman People could be induced to confer commands by its own action, and the process of finding generals for jobs was apt to induce the parallel process of finding jobs for generals. These special commands are often called illegal, but that is hardly the word—they were exceptional and often justified. But the senatorial convention, like most ageing conventions, was allergic to the exceptional. It is too much to say that men who held such commands constantly imposed their will upon the State by the threat of force. What is true is that, though the Republic defended and increased its place in the world, it did it by risking that constitutional stability which was predominantly a civilian affair.

Within ten years of Sulla's abdication the part of his work that meant most for senatorial authority was undone. Was it possible by any other means to preserve the convention of aristocratic government through the Senate or to find some other form of government which would ensure internal peace and stability?

The Romans were great lawyers, but they were not political philosophers. The nearest thing they knew to a political ideal was a harmonious balance of magistrates, Senate and People with the Senate as the chief factor. But the times were too unharmonious, the forces too easily unbalanced; the Senate's authority had been undermined. The one contemporary political observer whose opinions we know fairly well is Cicero, who was versed in Greek political speculation and in the tradition of Roman history. During his consulship he had believed, not without cause, that Rome was threatened by an anarchist plot led by Catiline. For the moment senators and *equites* had joined forces to defend property and the State, while the mass of the Roman People applauded. So Cicero dreamed of a Concord of the two Orders[18]—the senators and *equites*—which might unite to secure and maintain what he called "Peace with dignity" (*Otium cum dignitate,*[19] *otium* meaning the absence of domestic strife, and *dignitas,* the satisfaction of legitimate ambition). But once the danger was past, there was not enough community of interest to keep the two Orders united, and there were too many claims to *dignitas* not to disturb *otium.*

So this hope was quickly refuted by events. Then, a dozen years afterwards, Cicero wrote his *De republica,* of which not all has survived.[20] His ideal state, which was to be what he believed Rome had been just before the Gracchi, would, he hoped, be guided by the wise counsel of statesmen, of whom he may have thought of himself as the leading example. The authority of the Senate might then be reinforced by his own authority. But, alas, to the high aristocrats Cicero was not of their kind. And though Cicero did not lack courage he was not a soldier, and the fighting nobility of Rome had little use for a civilian Pericles or even for a civilian Solon. And however intelligent Cicero might be, he had his illusions, and what, in the end, the nobles wanted was not *his* wisdom but *their* way. It is possible, though far from certain, that Cicero also dreamed of the stability of the State being shielded by an eminent soldier. The reputation of the great Pompey would match the task, but his career had not shown him wholly loyal to the senatorial tradition. Nor did the aristocrats wholly trust him. Cicero himself did not wholly trust him either, and it is hard to think that Pompey, despite his administrative capacity, had the political insight needed for such a role.

There was one other possibility, though this did not appeal to Cicero, that a coalition of powerful men with their followers might bring stability to the State. Such a coalition, conventionally called by historians the First Triumvirate, was formed of Pompey the most famous of soldiers, Crassus the richest of financiers, and Caesar the most adroit of politicians. But to give stability to the State the coalition must itself be stable, and it was not. The members of the coalition must devote themselves continuously to the task, and they did not. Pompey and Crassus never trusted each other, and Caesar, after being consul, went off to conquer Gaul in ten years of hard fighting.

Crassus perished making war on the Parthians; the one link of affection between Caesar and Pompey was broken by the untimely death of Caesar's daughter, who was Pompey's beloved wife. As Caesar's reputation grew, Pompey became jealous of him, and a coalition of three became a rivalry of two. In Gaul Caesar had learned to be the autocratic general of a strong army, and the ruling classes feared his ambition. They tried to thwart his hopes of a second consulship to be followed —presumably—by another great command. The jealousy of Pompey and the fears of the aristocrats drew them together. They may have misjudged Caesar, who may have wanted nothing more, though nothing less, than the due promotion of his own *dignitas*. But when Caesar found that the constitution was to be worked against him and not for him, to be used to deny him what be believed to be his right and to end his career, he marched into Italy. In a hard-fought war he defeated his enemies and made himself the master of the Roman State by force. He became in Rome the autocrat he had learned to be in Gaul. He was a second Sulla, though clement where Sulla had been cruel, but he had not Sulla's readiness to remodel the State and then leave it to run itself. He was credited with the dictum that Sulla had been an innocent when he abdicated.[21]

For some two or three years Roman politics simply stopped. To Caesar the Senate which had contained his enemies meant nothing; the tribunate meant an exasperating survival, the more exasperating because he had affected to be its champion; the People meant an avenue to power that had outlived its usefulness now power was his; the magistrates were, in effect, his nominees, and the agents of his will. That was Rome under Caesar's autocracy. How he meant to mould the Roman State to be the vehicle of his will no one can say for certain—at least I can't say for certain. We know what he was like as a soldier,[22] for he has told us and some of his lieutenants have told us too. He was, like Napoleon, a mixture of general planning and particular improvisation and it may be that, with years, improvisation gained on planning. He had become the spirit of intellectual pride in a community that had for centuries believed that only in a multitude of counsellors there was wisdom. So far as I can see, he was content, for the moment, to promote the dictatorship, that is emergency power, to a system.[23] But as the forms of the Republic still remained, it seemed to men who were loyal to forms that, with Caesar removed, the Republic would come into its own again. His profound egotism provoked the egotism of others. His clemency, his efficiency, his genius did not, to sincere Republicans, justify his monopoly of power. And the plain truth is that his *dignitas* took up too much

room, and left too little room for the *dignitas* of others. Whatever his ultimate plans may have been, he had not as yet created
a monarchy, but at most an autocracy which, it seemed, would
only perish with him. The answer was simple: what the sword
had given him, the dagger could take from him. And on the
Ides of March it did.

The Ides of March was the climax of the Age of Revolution
but it was not its end: in fact it continued for half a generation
more. Whatever the conspirators may have hoped, the old
order did not return and their act was not final: if the assassination, said Macbeth, could trammel up the consequence and
could achieve, with his surcease, success—if. And assassina-
tions often suffer from a serious disadvantage: it is hard to make
them pass off smoothly. And the murder of Caesar raised more
problems than it solved.

In theory, it is true, the dictatorship was a kind of inter-
lude or episode which, when ended, left the constitutional
machine as it was before. But Caesar had been no ordinary
dictator: he had made and was making, at the moment of his
death, many arrangements, partly to control the State, partly
to improve its working, partly to reward his adherents. For,
as Professor Syme has pointed out in his *Roman Revolution*,
there was a Caesarian party in the sense that a host of men had
linked their fortunes with his. Though some had turned against
him, many believed in his star, if only because they had hitched
their wagons to it. And his veterans cared for their general a
good deal more than they cared for the Republic. The acts of
Caesar could not be revoked without producing chaos: the
consul in Rome was his lieutenant Antony; his great nephew
Octavian, his adoptive son by his will, dared to claim his name
and his inheritance. Both could appeal to Caesar's veterans.
Cicero, who in the last year of his life showed great energy and

no small political skill, led an attempt to give the old reality to the rule of the Senate, and to play off Octavian against Antony. But as against the aristocrats who had killed Caesar, and Cicero who tried to restore the old order of things, Antony and Octavian were bound in the end to work together, and at last they did. A new coalition, what is called the Second Triumvirate, was formed. Antony and Octavian added to themselves a third, Lepidus, who had an army worth buying in, an army worth more than his own scanty talents.

The dictatorship had been outlawed after Caesar's death. But the Second Triumvirate was really a dictatorship in commission. It was, what the so-called First Triumvirate was not, constituted by an act of state with a defined task, to reconstitute the State, and for a defined period of five years (though in fact it was later renewed). But that was a façade.[24] Its power, in fact, rested on armies, and its first purpose was the destruction of its enemies and the avenging of Caesar. In a proscription and a second civil war its enemies were destroyed, among them Cicero, and then, at Philippi, Caesar was avenged on the men of the Ides of March. Beneath the shadow of the Triumvirate the ordinary processes of government were performed by men really appointed by it. But it was an alliance of ambitious men. When a son of Pompey raised fleets to dominate the Western Mediterranean it first bargained with him and then crushed him. Lepidus was turned out of the Triumvirate, and Octavian and Antony became the military rulers, the one of the West, the other of the East. Octavian assumed the championship of Western Roman ideas, Antony with Cleopatra went Hellenistic as a ruler, though he remained a Roman general at the head of Roman legions. There did not seem to be room in the world for both Octavian and Antony, unless the Mediterranean world broke into two. That break was averted by the victory of

Octavian over Antony; Octavian triumphed in the name of Rome, Italy and the West and rapidly brought the Eastern half of the empire under his control. The way was clear for a new political experiment. Two civil wars and a proscription had gone far to empty the political stage, and Octavian and his followers took in hand what had been in name the commission of the Second Triumvirate, namely the reconstitution of the Roman State. It was, at the least, a New Deal.

V

AUGUSTUS PRINCEPS

THE EMINENT PHILOSOPHER A. N. Whitehead in his *Adventures of Ideas* quotes Edmund Burke's famous outburst: "For heaven's sake, satisfy *somebody*" and goes on to say that governments are best classified by considering who are the "somebodies" they are in fact endeavouring to satisfy.[1] This is not a very philosophic approach to political ideas, though it has affinities with political practice. But it is not irrelevant to our inquiry. If, to begin with, we consider the origin and duration of Augustus' Principate in terms of the people it satisfied, we shall after all be applying the criterion of a great Roman jurist, *cui bono?* What in fact did various sorts of people desire and hope for when the Principate began, and how far did Augustus satisfy their hopes and desires? The Roman People in general wanted peace, security from civil war and a privileged position in the world. These Augustus secured for it. The Roman aristocracy—what remained of it—wanted a share in the government but—weakened and shaken in nerve as it was—no more than a share, together with respect for the Senate, the embodiment, or at least the symbol, of the aristocracy. This Augustus left to it.[2] The *equites* desired the opportunity of securing their position and prosperity by the exercise of their aptitude for commerce and financial management. This opportunity he gave to them.[3] Augustus' friends, who had linked their fortunes with his, hoped for successful careers, and their

hopes were gratified. The legions—we may assume—wished
not to fight other legions, though they were very ready to
fight the enemies of Rome. And they wanted to be sure of their
pay while they stayed with the eagles, and when they had
earned their discharge they wanted to be sure of grants of land
and money, the ancient counterpart of pensions. All this
Augustus provided for them, after he had reduced the existing
legions, his own and Antony's, from about seventy-five to
about twenty-eight. With these legions, and a roughly equiva-
lent force of auxiliary troops recruited in the provinces, he met
the military needs of the Empire.

These—the Roman People, the senatorial aristocracy, the
equites, Augustus' friends or partisans, the legions—were the
people who were bound to come first in the mind of a man
concerned to remodel the Roman community and not uncon-
cerned with his own career, power, and, indeed, safety. But
there were other people in the world whose satisfaction would
at least make his task easier as well as more beneficent. The
provinces may well have hoped to be better governed, the
client kings and princes to find in Rome a steady protector, and
both may have hoped not to face again the burdens that a
Roman civil war had laid upon most of them. They were not
to be disappointed. In short—to return to Whitehead's formula
—the people whom the Augustan Principate endeavoured to
satisfy were pretty nearly everybody who mattered.

It is, no doubt, easier to do for people what they want done
than what they do not want done. Even so, it was a great
task, and Augustus showed notable skill and diligence in
achieving it. Though, indeed, he was not singlehanded: in
Agrippa[4] he had a loyal general and a military organizer of the
first distinction, who, it may be supposed, did most to carry
through the great demobilization that followed the Civil War,

and then planned imperial strategy. Soon there appeared in Augustus' stepsons, Drusus and Tiberius, two skilful soldiers. In his domestic minister, Maecenas,[5] he had an adroit manager of men and of affairs. And among his followers he found new-made aristocrats of office to supplement what remained of the old nobility, who, most of them, also served the New Order. Augustus himself, of a thrifty Italian stock, was his own finance minister, endowed by the wealth of Egypt and the Ptolemies he had overthrown, so that he could eke out the resources of the public Treasury. And he could call upon the financial skill of the Equestrian Order throughout the Empire, as he could use the administrative and military capacity of the senators. But, even so, it was a great task, diligently, resourcefully and unobtrusively performed.

What I have just described is, in the main, more a matter of administration—the use of the powers which Augustus received and the simple practical reasons why he was able to achieve his purpose. We may now turn to consider the constitutional and political setting of the Principate, which is the traditional name for the New Order in the State.

After Octavian—to use for the moment the convenient name applied to him by historians before he became Augustus —had returned to Rome, with Antony defeated and the kingdom of Cleopatra conquered, he became consul along with Agrippa, and the two in the year 28 B.C. appeared as equal colleagues on the old model. To conduct the war, which was officially directed against Egypt, Octavian had had powers which united under his leadership Italy and the Western provinces. The war was over in January, 29 B.C.: the temple of Janus was closed to show that the world was at peace. And these special powers of Octavian would end with the outbreak of peace. These powers he renounced so far as they were more than the expression of trust in him. The Second Triumvirate was already a thing of the past. A Triumvirate of two after the retirement of Lepidus is a strain on faith, a Triumvirate of one after the death of Antony is a strain on reason. And so, in the year 28, in theory Rome had returned to the old order of the Republic. But the old order had ended in civil war. Next year at latest there would return to Rome a general of the old nobility who had won resounding victories on the Danube. Could Rome afford the old competition for power? I conjecture that in 28 B.C. Octavian was offered and accepted control of the whole State,[6] but only because he meant to discard part of this control. He was, I imagine, shrewd enough to know that in the game of politics it is best to discard from strength. There were no doubt pourparlers between the old hands in the Senate and Octavian, and in January, 27 B.C., Octavian, as he says in his own account of his career, "transferred the State from his own control of it (or power over it) to the free decision (the *arbitrium*) of the Senate and People of Rome". This means the Senate and People were to take the responsibility of deciding how the State should henceforward be governed.[7] The Senate, presumably with the ratification of the People, invested him for a period of ten years with the complete control of almost all the provinces where there was need of an army. Octavian would go on being consul, and at the same time he would be responsible for the greater part of the Empire, appointing governors and generals. The first danger, that of civil war, was averted by the simple expedient of putting almost all the legions under the orders of one man. For it takes two to make a civil war. Then the name "Augustus", the name by which I shall henceforward refer to him, was conferred on him. It was a name of vague religious dignity which did not challenge the ancient aristocratic names of Rome, because it was on a different, if higher, plane. A golden shield was set up inscribed with the four cardinal virtues which were attributed to him—his valour, his clemency, his justice, his piety.[8] The truth was that in his advance to power he had displayed certain other qualities. He had been a resolute and ruthless careerist, and even the filial piety that avenged his adoptive father Caesar—while genuine enough—had served his own ambition, the promotion of his own *dignitas*. His clemency was now real, if perforce limited to those of his opponents he had brought himself to spare. I say "perforce limited" because I remind myself of the brigand who on his deathbed was adjured to forgive his enemies, and replied: "Yes, father, but how can I? I have shot them all." His justice and his valour had been proved by the arbitrament of war and the goodness of his cause. These golden virtues he was to justify, and meanwhile everyone knew that he was the first man in the State, and that its peace, safety and happiness were best secured if he was and remained that. No one wanted freedom if it only meant freedom to indulge in faction, misgovernment and, perhaps, civil war. If he had worn the velveteens of the old poacher, he now assumed the decorous livery of the new gamekeeper.

Augustus was consul in each of the next few years and at the same time he managed in person or through his lieutenants the provinces assigned to him, while the other provinces remained in the care of the Senate. But this settlement had its inconveniences—the ablest of men could not be in two places at once, the consulship was a prize the moiety of which one man should not monopolize every year, and in 23 B.C. Augustus abandoned the consulship though he retained his great provincial command.

At the same time it was declared that his proconsular *imperium*—which was already directly exercised in his own

provinces—ranked as greater than the proconsular power of
those who governed the provinces still left in the care of the
Senate.[9] This declaration meant that in his own provinces his
power remained what it was—the direct exercise of a control
that was vested in him at all times, and in all matters, while
in the other provinces his will would prevail when and where
he cared to assert it.[10] It did not mean that he took over the
government of these other—the senatorial—provinces, but that
he had the first (and only) word in his own provinces and the
last word in the others. In Rome itself, though he now ceased
to be elected consul year by year, he was given prerogatives that
would prevent the fact that he was not consul hampering his
influence upon policy or diminishing his dignity and prestige.[11]
For good reasons he abandoned an office, but retained the
reality of power.

The proconsular *imperium* of Augustus was granted him for
periods of years, though, in fact, its renewal was inevitably
automatic. But he also needed to be raised above possible
hindrances to steady control and initiation of domestic policy
in Rome. He could be sure of the Senate, in which, indeed, he
had been named the first senator, *Princeps Senatus,* for he really
controlled most of its membership. He could be sure of the
magistrates of the whole People, for he had the privilege to
commend men for election, and his commendation, where he
exercised it, made their election a foregone conclusion. What
was really an urban police force,[12] with his Praetorian Guard
handy at need, ensured that public disorder could no longer
interrupt the orderly processes of government. There remained
the ancient institution of the tribunate, which had, on occasion,
been so disturbing or paralysing a force in the politics of the
last decades of the Republic. It had become an endemic disease
in the body politic, and Augustus applied to it what may be

called a homoeopathic remedy. Roman constitutional practice permitted the enjoyment of the powers of an office without its actual possession. Augustus was therefore granted, not the office of tribune, which, incidentally, as a patrician and not a plebeian, he could not hold, but the use of its powers. He was not a colleague of the annually elected tribunes; they could not challenge him as one of themselves. His tribunician power meant on the positive side that he could do what any tribune or group of tribunes could do, and, on the negative side, prevent any tribune or group of tribunes from doing anything he did not wish them to do. Such was its practical effect, and it had an ideological claim. For it did not abolish an institution so firmly rooted in prescription, it did not deny the right of the Commons to have their special representation; it could be described as raising the People's rights to a higher power;[13] but, in practice, that higher power was vested in his will. The notion that Julius Caesar had once had such a power is, I think, untenable:[14] it was a characteristic invention of Augustus, a subtle application of unobtrusive common sense to a recalcitrant problem.

I ended the last chapter with the observation that the new order was, at least, a New Deal. It was—with the same cards, plus some jokers. This was the most valuable joker which Augustus added to his hand. It became the practice to reckon the years of his Principate by the years of his tribunician power—for though it was granted for life, it was formally reconferred each year and, so far as this reckoning had a monarchical air, it was in terms of the annually renewed representation of the People's rights.

This settlement of the year 23 marks the practical consolidation of Augustus' position as the governing factor in the State. It may be that four years later he received some additional prerogatives of a consular character, but essentially he had now what he needed in the way of power.[15]

The inscription in which Augustus records the achievements of his long life contains a famous sentence. From the time when he was named Augustus onwards he had, he says, "no more power than his colleagues in each magistracy that he held".[16] This means that when he was consul his magisterial power was no greater than that of his fellow consul. It may also mean that the same was true when, as happened on five occasions, another man at his request was made his colleague in the possession of the tribunician power.[17] But his equality with a colleague in the consulship was more formal than real, and his equality with a colleague in the tribunician power may not always have been even formally true, if his colleague only exercised the power for a particular task or within a particular part of the Empire. We may suspect that the words I have quoted are where they are in order to lead up to the words that follow them, the words "but I surpassed all men in *auctoritas*". This he did because he was *princeps*, and he was *princeps* because he did. *Auctoritas* and *princeps* were in so far linked together, but that does not mean that his *auctoritas* was the sole ingredient in his position, which could be compendiously described as that of *princeps*, the first man in the State. But they may be considered together.

It was the fact that he was the *princeps* that has given the name Principate to the first two centuries and more of the Roman Empire. Both these political ideas—the idea of *auctoritas* and the idea of the *princeps*—had already been anticipated to some extent in the Republic. Under the Republic a leading statesman might be said to possess *auctoritas,* but, what was more than that, as we have seen, *auctoritas* was the characteristic possession of the Senate in the heyday of the Senate's influence.[18] Now, in the Augustan Principate, while the Senate remained in dignified security as a junior or sometimes sleeping partner of the *princeps*, its effective *auctoritas* really passed to Augustus. And rightly so, inasmuch as men now looked to him for the initiative, guidance and leadership which the Senate had supplied. And also under the Republic leading statesmen had been called *principes*, and the senior (or leading) senator had been the *princeps* of the Senate.[19] Augustus was now *princeps* of the Senate, a fact which lent a share of his own prestige to that eminent body. But also he was *princeps* par excellence in the whole State, and not for a time, but admittedly for all the time. And in practice *auctoritas* was more than a kind of personal quality—it was a source of decision supplementing and at need transcending other sources of decision. And *princeps* in the person of Augustus reflected not an office nor a group of powers but an admitted primacy to which other men could yield without loss of self-respect, without becoming no more than the courtiers of a monarch. There was to be a time when emperors became more aloof, their house more a palace, and their palace almost sacred, but that time was still in the future. To attend upon a great man was already a social convention, and so far a social convention sufficed.

When we compare the authority—the *auctoritas*—of the Senate of the Middle Republic with the authority or the *auctoritas* of Augustus, we have to remember that the *auctoritas* of the Senate was not reinforced and protected by positive legally secured powers.[20] It might settle this or that, but not with the *imperium* or *potestas* of a magistrate; it might make policy but it could not carry it out with plenary executive power; it was an advisory body and it was not made anything else by the fact that its advice was almost always taken. It could be challenged by tribunes and by magistrates, by veto or legisla-

tion. It guided rather than ruled, however much its guidance
was followed without demur at the zenith of its authority.

On the other hand, the *auctoritas* of Augustus was reinforced
and protected by legally conferred powers[21]—his proconsular
imperium in his own provinces, his legally secured superior
imperium in senatorial provinces when he chose to use it,
certain legally secured prerogatives within the city, and his
legally conferred tribunician power. This formidable combination of powers secured against all comers the potent exercise
of his *auctoritas*. It is true to say that his *auctoritas* made men
ready to see his will prevail, his positive active powers precluded
men from doing anything else.

This does not mean that he was an autocrat whose autocracy
left no one freedom of action or constitutional rights and
powers, but he was the *princeps*, the admitted first man in the
State and that not only by the pre-eminence of his personality
but by the pre-eminence of his power. His legal powers were
defined and conferred by Senate and People, his *auctoritas* was
not defined nor conferred: it was accepted without challenge.
It is true that his proconsular *imperium* was for periods and
subject to renewal, his tribunician power was renewed year by
year, and the People, if they could confer it, could, in theory,
refuse to confer it. But the alternative to renewal was so daunt-
ing a prospect that it is hard to believe it could ever be seriously
contemplated.

The Principate of Augustus was entrenched in the hopes and
fears of men, and it was morally justified by its over-all
results. Its powers did not reach this secure pre-eminence in
a moment, but by a series of acts of state registering the will
of the Senate and People, at each stage justified by the interest
of the State and not arbitrarily imposed by the *princeps*:[22] his
auctoritas was a thing of growth. If he surpassed all men in it

when he had been named Augustus, he surpassed all men more
and more as his long reign proceeded. The length of Augustus'
reign consolidated the power of his position and the order of
things his Principate replaced passed out of memory—when he
died some forty years after he became Augustus, "how few
men were left who had seen the Republic".²³ When all deductions are made, the over-all beneficence of his reign had endowed the New Order with an ample good will. Probably
early in his rule he published an edict in which he expressed
the hope that it might be vouchsafed to him to establish the
State so safe and sound that he might enjoy the reward he
sought—to be named the author of the best order of things and
that when he died he might die in the hope that the foundation
of the Commonwealth that he had laid might abide un-
moved.²⁴ These aspirations were fulfilled: by what seems to
have been a spontaneous demonstration of public good will
and recognition sixteen years before his death he was solemnly
named Father of his Country—*pater patriae*, and this, I imagine,
seemed to him the crowning moment of his career. This is
what he says: "When I was in my thirteenth consulship (i.e. in
2 B.C.) the Senate and the Equestrian Order and the whole
Roman People gave me the name of Father of my Country and
decreed that this title should be engraved upon the porch of
my house and in the Senate House, and in the Forum Augustum
beneath the quadriga set up in my honour by decree of the
Senate."²⁵ This fits its place at the end of his own account of
his achievements. I would not think it is necessary to find in
the phrase "*pater patriae*" the expression of a new *mystique* or a
hint of kingship.²⁶ It is rather just what most people had come
to think about Augustus, and I would quote words that put
this as I think it should be put: "Most people in the Western
World, disregarding constitutional niceties, thought of Augus-

tus as chief among citizens, as the head of the Roman People".[27]
And, when he died, the Principate passed to Tiberius in cir-
cumstances that suggest it was, as it were, laid like a wreath on
Augustus' coffin, to be then assumed as a crown by his successor.

I have spoken of the aspirations of Augustus, but this does
not mean that he was a man of saintly self-abnegation. It would
be idle to deny that he came first in his own scale of things, and
that though he sought no more power than he needed, he
sought it with resolution and without scruple. A close study of
his own account of his career suggests that he did not set himself to tell the whole truth and nothing but the truth. It has
been said that the inscription on a tombstone is not a deposition
upon oath, and much the same is true of most autobiographies.
His was a complex character and with its complexities we are
not concerned. What is more relevant is the question how far
he was governed by the ideals and doctrines of political
philosophy. The idea that he found in Cicero's *De republica* a
justification of a kind of monarchy does not match what can
be deduced from what remains of that work nor does it match
what can be deduced from his own acts and words.[28] It would
be unjust to deny to him, once he had attained power, a sense
of duty and a sincere belief that he was creating a New Order
that transcended the satisfaction of his own *dignitas*. In this
sense of duty he may have been inspired, at first or second hand,
by the doctrines of the Stoics. But he might well have done
just what he did, had neither Cicero nor the Stoics ever existed.
He appealed to Roman ideas and Roman sentiments and
sought to conjure the sense of religious guilt evoked in the
Romans by the Civil Wars. In this too he appears sincere, and
in his efforts to reform Roman morals he went further than his
own interests demanded and went beyond the sentiment of

Roman society of his day. That he cared for respectability does not make him a hypocrite, nor does the fact that at need he dissembled the degree of his personal power.

It is true that, as his Principate proceeded, the Senate and People of Rome counted for less and the *princeps* counted for more. The famous doctrine that the Principate was a dyarchy of *princeps* and Senate goes beyond the evidence. The evidence does not indicate a division of power but rather a division of labour. Augustus was at pains to make the Senate fit to take a share in government, he treated it with respect as an institution and used senators in almost all high tasks and dignified positions and came to admit a committee of senators to his counsels. What the Senate could do, it did, but, as time went on, there was a continuous drift of responsibility from Senate to *princeps*. He was, too, the first man in the Senate, and lent to it a due portion of his own prestige. And it is not ever difficult for a body, so highly placed, so rich in memories, to underrate the extent to which its effective powers are on the ebb.

The Roman People remained a vehicle of power even if, as time went on, Augustus guided the vehicle more and more. It was still invoked in legislation and associated with the Senate in the conferment of his powers. Until late in his Principate it elected the magistrates, but with deference to the wishes of the *princeps* when he thought fit to command candidates for its choice. And before his Principate ended, as is now known, this right was anticipated to the point of decision through what was called *designatio* by a college of senators and *equites*.[29] And a partial compensation for this diversion of effective power was granted to citizens residing in the city in the election of municipal officers so that they had some real responsibility, if on a lower plane.

Finally, Augustus did not jealously monopolize power. There are instances of his causing to be conferred on others at times the proconsular *imperium* and the tribunician power which were the very foundations of his positive control of the State. One thing which he did not, and could not, share was his *auctoritas,* and he was bound to remain the first man in the State whoever was the second. As far as there was anything monarchical in his position the conferment of similar powers on anyone else did not divide the monarchy but supplemented or extended it.

Some have seen in Augustus a military autocrat, like a Hellenistic king who was, above all else, *tête d'armée.* It is true that, for all practical purposes, the Roman army was his to command. It is also true that, were this not so, his position would be more than precarious. But he was not the creation of the army, and he never promoted it to be more than a servant of the State. The President of the United States is the Commander in Chief of the armed forces of the Union, but he is not chosen by the armed forces and no one would suppose him a military autocrat.

It may, none the less, be debated whether Rome was a monarchy or a Republic during the Principate of Augustus. It is certainly true that his positive powers were Republican in origin. They were derived from the Senate and People of Rome or from the Senate acting for both. So far as his powers went beyond the normal practice of the Republic these were due to an act of the Republic making a temporary and partial abdication of powers which, *in theory*, still remained its own. Such was the *theory*, but the fact remained that Augustus' powers could not be terminated without throwing the whole mechanism of government into confusion. These powers were acquired in stages, and at each stage they seemed no more than fitted the practical needs of the State and the desires of its citizens. Herein was displayed the notable constitutional tact of the first *princeps*.

The answer to the question whether Rome was a monarchy or a Republic is composite. It was not a dyarchy of Republic and monarchy if that means a partnership in power at all times and in all places. In Rome and Italy the government was Republican in theory and, in most matters, Republican in practice. In the Empire at large, in the provinces placed in the direct control of the *princeps* it was Republican in theory but monarchical in practice, for Augustus appointed the governors and they were responsible to him. In the provinces left in the care of the Senate it was Republican in theory and normally Republican in practice—normally because of the possible incidence of Augustus' overriding power. As time went on the motive force was more and more derived from the rule of the *princeps*. If I may be forgiven a somewhat frivolous analogy, it will be of an automobile: the parts were Republican, but the *princeps* increasingly supplied the gasoline that made it go, the oil that made it go smoothly and the water that kept it cool.

Now to return to the theme with which I started this chapter. The political practice of the Augustan Principate with its subtle adaptation of old ideas and infiltrations of new ones is what we are particularly concerned with for the purpose of these lectures. But what mattered more to the world of Augustus' own day was its peace, its security and the economic progress that these made possible, the concentration of the great practical ability of the Romans on the tasks of government for the good of both governed and government. The prime agent of all this was a man who added to great diligence and capacity the advantage of being, if not a very great man, at least the man the world needed. It seemed that with the

Augustan Principate the world had reached an equilibrium which it was the universal interest to maintain. There had been no such violent break with the past as would offend Roman conservatism. There remained room for careers but careers limited to the needs of the State and Empire, and though the *princeps* may have become too much an earthly Providence,[30] though initiative might flag, the Augustan Principate did, at the least, give the Mediterranean world release from old fears and old troubles and a new hope for the future.

Before we leave the topic of the establishment of the Principate there is one thing more which calls for mention, for it both affects and reveals the attitude of Rome, Italy and the Provinces towards the *princeps*, the head of the State, and is a particular manifestation of the sentiments which I have been describing. This topic may compendiously be described as ruler cult.[31]

No one would assert that Augustus or his immediate successors ruled by a divine sanction. But in the Eastern half of the Empire, there had existed a cult of royalty associated with the idea that kings were benefactors or saviours. In that part of the Empire Augustus was the nearest thing in sight to a king who was both. The provincials and client princes had already, here and there, made Rome and some eminent Romans an object of cult. They were now permitted to place Augustus by the side of Rome. This had three effects that may be, in part, political. It carried forward into the New Order ideas from the Old, it allowed the recognition of what may be called quasi-godhead by benefaction, and it turned into a convenient channel any religious ideas that had been connected with the State. On the other hand, Roman citizens in these Eastern provinces were restricted to the cult of Rome and the deified Julius Caesar, a patron saint at least in Heaven, whatever he had been on earth.

In the West the provincials were also permitted to have a cult of Rome and Augustus, but this was not the continuation of old ideas, for in the West, apart from the Kingdom of Numidia, ruler cult was not at home. Here the cult, which first appears for certain in Gaul more than a decade after Augustus had become *princeps*, may well be due to deliberate policy—to enhance the loyalty of the Gallic notables who served the cult, and to link it with loyalty to Rome as well as to Augustus.

In Italy and especially in Rome it was against tradition to turn a living man into a god. If those are right who think that this tradition was broken in the lifetime of Caesar, on the Ides of March the tradition had been avenged. The worship of the deified Caesar, Divus Julius, was a posthumous worship, and Augustus was in no hurry to attain posthumous honours. The partial approximation to cult that is found in the institution of the Augustales, an association open to freedmen,[32] may have been due to the desire to give some dignity to that respectable freedman stratum for which society, as Augustus saw it, had a place. Humble people were encouraged to associate him with their domestic worship, though this did not mean they treated him as a god. In the camps of the armies the military loyalty to Augustus might add a representation of the ruling *princeps* to the standards, but these are a focus of loyalty rather than the object of direct worship.[33] Poets and other men of letters, or private persons in private dedications, might use the language of compliment or mythology to declare Augustus to be the manifestation or representative of a god on earth,[34] but that did not remove him from humanity, though it might be the earnest of divinity after death. There were prayers *for* him—and you do not pray *for* a god—*ex hypothesi* a god does not need to be prayed *for*. There were also celebrations of his birthday and so on—but in the British Commonwealth the Queen's Birthday is not a Festival of the Church, nor, I believe, in the United States is the Birthday of the President.

So far then as there was ruler worship associated with Augustus or his immediate successors, it did not give divine sanction to the Principate, nor was divine sanction needed to secure the succession. Ruler cult, that is to say, was not something that made a *princeps*: it was rather an attitude towards a *princeps* the basis of whose power was secular and not religious. What it expressed, above all, was a grateful sense of favours past and a lively sense of favours to come. It was not the bringing in of the next world to redress the balance of this: at the most, it was the bringing in of the next world to maintain the balance of this.

VI

THE DEVELOPMENT
OF THE PRINCIPATE

THE MAIN THEME of the last chapter was the establishment of the Principate, which produced a New Order in which men rejoiced to feel secure. But if this happy state of things was to continue, one thing more was needed—the Principate should continue.[1] Granted that almost everyone would wish it to survive the death of its founder, this could only happen if someone became *princeps* and that meant that he must enjoy the powers on which, in fact, the position of the *princeps* had come to rest. These powers were not, in law or logic, anything that Augustus could bequeath to another in his will as he could bequeath his personal property or as a Hellenistic king could bequeath his kingdom. They were his to use, not his to confer, and they disappeared with his death. But he might so arrange matters that their conferment upon a man of his choice would be almost inevitable. And, indeed, in the year before his death, all these powers were conferred on Tiberius, and Augustus' death did not, and could not, cancel their conferment.

But what about his *auctoritas,* which Augustus possessed by the admitted force of his personality, by his pre-eminence in character, achievement and service to the State? Judged by this criterion Agrippa too had earned a claim to *auctoritas* in his own right by virtue of his services to the State, and had Augustus died, as he nearly did, in the year 23 B.C., it would seem that Agrippa was the next best, and so the next, *princeps*, if the New Order was to continue. And the New Order, then so new, was most secure if a man of admitted eminence and ability was ready to foster its growth should the founder ascend to Heaven. But Augustus did not die in 23; instead, after eleven years Agrippa died, and there was no one else who was, as yet, of his stature. And he had been the husband of Augustus' one child, Julia. Now Augustus' stepson Tiberius was caused to set aside the wife he cared for and marry Julia. Thus he became like Agrippa. Moreover, he, too, was making a name for himself as a soldier, and had the beginnings of a reputation of his own. He received the tribunician power and may have seemed to be growing up to be, as it were, the next Agrippa, the natural successor in the Principate. But this was not the only side to the matter: Augustus had a truly Roman predilection for members of his own Julian family, and adopted the two young sons of his daughter by Agrippa. They were advanced, and marked out by being named the leaders of the aristocracy of the rising generation.[2] And Tiberius withdrew into a voluntary exile. It is not clear that the two young princes, C. and L. Caesar, possessed the capacity to match their apparent destiny, and they died before they could show they did.[3] Their death was, as his own words show,[4] a bitter grief to Augustus, whose affection for them may well have overborne his political insight and his sense of responsibility. There was a reluctant reconciliation between him and Tiberius, who returned to share the burden of rule, to become, in effect, *consors imperii* of Augustus. He was, what Agrippa had been, beyond doubt the second man in the Commonwealth. And the fact that Augustus now clearly meant Tiberius to take his place as *princeps* was a fact of political, if not of strictly constitutional, significance. The memory of free competition for leadership in the State was a dim and unpleasant memory. The machine of government had been geared to a single will and would break down if it was ungeared.

With a cautious and scrupulous regard for constitutional proprieties Tiberius allowed greatness to be thrust upon him. This was done by a Senate which knew first that the choice must lie between the Principate and anarchy—a choice that was easy; and second that if there was to be a *princeps*, the *princeps* must be Tiberius. Tiberius was now an elderly man, rather distrustful of himself and more distrustful of others, a true member of his ancient family, the Claudians, with their hard pride and intolerant realism. He accepted power as a burden, a burden which, as he may well have said, only the mind of Augustus had the capacity to bear.[5] Tacitus describes the scene in the first book of his *Annals*[6] as a revealing of hypocrisy in Tiberius and servility in the Senate: but it was really far more a combination of common sense on the part of the Senate and a reluctant response to his duty on the part of Tiberius.

But, able as Tiberius was, he had become sourly grim, prone to suspicion, unlovable. The good relations between the *princeps* and the aristocracy broke down, though the government of the Empire remained efficient. His nephew and adopted son Germanicus died young, as did his own son Drusus. Tiberius may have seen in Sejanus a helper such as Augustus had found first in Agrippa and then in himself, but he was disillusioned and Sejanus perished. In his latest years he did not mark out and train a successor.[7] And then, lonely and aloof, he died. But it had by now become clear that the machine of government could do its work without a *princeps* of great capacity and experience such as Tiberius and his predecessor had been. What mattered politically was to avoid a struggle for the succession, and Gaius, often called Caligula, was made *princeps* as the handiest member of the Julio-Claudian family. He started with the advantage of being at least unlike what Tiberius had become. But power turned his weak head. He soon outstayed his welcome and was assassinated. At this moment it looked as if it was an open question if the Principate should continue and if so under whom. The Senate may, for the moment, have forgotten that there was still a member of the Julio-Claudian family. But Gaius had an uncle, who was hiding behind a curtain till pulled out by a member of the Praetorian Guard, whose fellow soldiers approved of Claudius because he was the son of a very popular general.

The Senate hastened to invest him with the powers of the *princeps*. Claudius was an odd, pedantic, longwinded man—the sort of man many people believe professors to be, if they have not been privileged to meet any. The most uxorious of men, he was poisoned by his fourth wife to make way for her son, Nero. Yet in the fourteen years that lay between the comic irony of his accession and the tragic irony of his death, Claudius greatly strengthened the machinery of government and showed much good sense and much beneficent activity.[8] But his youthful successor Nero, once he escaped from his tutors, who had governed well in his name, outraged Roman sentiment. He behaved like a Greek virtuoso instead of like a Roman aristocrat. He murdered his mother and his stepbrother. More than that, he drove his best general to suicide, and this naturally alarmed the other generals. He forfeited the loyalty of the armies and, with it, the material safeguard of his power. At last the abundant stock of good will with which Augustus had endowed the Julio-Claudian family was exhausted. There followed what is called the Year of the Four Emperors—Galba, Otho, Vitellius and Vespasian. Otho disposed of Galba, Vitellius disposed of Otho, Vespasian disposed of Vitellius and survived without a rival. What then was to be done to get stability? This raises the next political question.

It was possible to confer on Vespasian the positive powers of a *princeps*—the proconsular *imperium* and the ·tribunician power. To these Augustus had added his *auctoritas*, and so, in a measure, had Tiberius; whereas Gaius, Claudius and Nero had the prestige of belonging, by birth or adoption, to Augustus' family, a kind of faint afterglow of his *auctoritas*. They thus enjoyed a sort of legitimacy which Vespasian did not possess. He was where he was by right of conquest and by that alone. What was needed was something more. The Senate produced a comprehensive decree duly confirmed by the people.[9] Of this decree the last part survives. It declared that Vespasian was entitled to do a number of things which Augustus, Tiberius and Claudius had been entitled to do.[10] But it went further: it added a clause which invoked the same precedents to confer on Vespasian "the right and power to do all such things as he may deem to serve the interests of the State, and the dignity of all things divine and human, public and private". Now this may be an attempt to define *auctoritas* (if the word define can be used of something so unlimited), and so to give to it a legal basis and substance, to make it something that can be conferred. The old order of things whereby the position of the *princeps* rested partly on legal commission, partly custom and partly the possession of *auctoritas* was altered. There is no longer a kind of compromise between Republican institutions and Imperial practice. There is the formal comprehensive recognition of the constitutional right of the *princeps* to be, in law as well as in fact, the ruler of the State.

However Vespasian had come to power, his position was now constitutionally secured. The system was a monarchy "in which", to quote the words of H. M. Last, "the monarch, not of compulsion but of choice, exposed himself to the force of educated opinion and so guided his actions that it should not be outraged. Of that opinion the foremost organ was the Senate"[11]—which indeed had for centuries been the effective day-to-day public opinion of Rome. When the relations between the *princeps* and the Senate were good, the *princeps* was more constitutional, when they were bad, the *princeps* was more autocratic. But, on the whole, despite some deviations towards autocracy, the settlement under Vespasian extended the period that can be called the Principate for well over a century.

Also Vespasian, though he owed his elevation to one of the great armies, was determined that when an army had settled that, it should not settle anything else. He was determined that the armies and the Praetorian Guard at Rome should not in the future be kingmakers but servants of the State. The Year of the Four Emperors, in which rival armies backed rival emperors, was an exception that proved the rule that prevailed till the Principate made way for a military autocracy. But the Principate was not—so it seems—made a hereditary monarchy by any formal action of the Senate. Vespasian did what he could to make up for this by declaring that his sons should reign after him, or no one.[12] These were not the only alternatives, but Vespasian's paternal and, at the same time, realistic mind saw no others. His two sons, Titus and Domitian, in turn succeeded him; it was a new dynasty, Flavian instead of Julio-Claudian. Domitian, though he did much for the Empire, came to hate the Senate and harried it, and was hated in return. How was the Senate to escape from the apparent dilemma propounded by Vespasian? It needed to remove Domitian and at the same time to provide for the successor. For by now there could be no question of a return to the Republic or to a free competition for power by force of arms.

Domitian was removed by the simple expedient of assassination. A successor was decided upon and was waiting, Nerva, a respectable senator who was an old man and with no son of his own. The army commanders had been won over, so far as they needed to be won over, and there was no new Year of the Four Emperors. Nerva was a transition to a new view of the office of *princeps* and of the succession to it. The new view was this. The right person to be *princeps* was to be the most suitable man for the task, regardless of his birth. The reigning *princeps* with the concurrence of the Senate was to discover who that was and mark him out for the succession by adoption. There had been a kind of precedent for this in the Hellenistic monarchies. In these the son of the king was marked out for the succession by being associated with the king as ruler. And, to come nearer home, Tiberius had been made a kind of colleague of Augustus in the last year of Augustus' reign. Thus when a reign ended there would be no conflict for power, and the Principate was in a way elective or, if you will, pre-elective. By this time everyone knew that the government must be monarchical in the sense that there was one man at the head of the State whose will could prevail over the will of everybody else. From this situation there was now no retreat, no return to a free Republic. Granted that plain fact, which doctrinaire Republicans might reject but could not alter, what was to be the moral basis of the *princeps*' position?

Under Vespasian, Titus and Domitian there had been a kind of ideological criticism of the Principate as being a dynastic autocracy. Now this ideology was conciliated. The *princeps* was now to be recognized as, above all, the first servant of the Community. This had been the philosophic justification provided for the Hellenistic monarchy, once it was established in the Successor kingdoms, and it could be made to fit the tenets of Stoicism, the dominant philosophy of the day. And, second, the claim that the *princeps* was freely chosen from everybody because he was the best man gave him a moral right to his position. The younger Pliny in his Panegyric on Nerva's successor, Trajan, uses the phrase, "He who is to rule over all ought to be chosen from all".[13] This is not the unassailable truism it sounds. When Dr. Johnson heard the line, "Who rules o'er freemen should himself be free", he made the comment, "It might as well be 'Who drives fat oxen should himself be fat'". But the idea behind Pliny's phrase is intelligible. For to be "the *best* man" should imply that *all* rival claims have been taken into account.

Well to return: Nerva adopted Trajan, a man of provincial birth, as "the best man" with the approval of the Senate, and on Nerva's death he duly assumed the duty of governing as not only *princeps* but as *optimus princeps*, as he was called.

Tacitus[14] declared that with Nerva two things had been reconciled which had not hitherto been reconcilable, viz. the Principate and Liberty. This really meant little more than that the Principate could be accepted without doing violence to people's self-respect. Trajan, then, ruled because he had been adopted and designated to succeed as being the best man for the task. He in turn in his last illness adopted Hadrian—for a like reason. At least Hadrian declared that Trajan had adopted him; whether this was a historical fact was doubted at the time and has been doubted since. The truth may be that Hadrian adopted Trajan as a father rather than that Trajan adopted Hadrian as a son. But, if the adoption was fictitious, Hadrian made it come true, and the principle remained unimpaired.

Hadrian, as he grew old and ill, repeated the process. His first choice didn't come to anything because the man chosen died. His second choice produced an excellent conscientious Emperor,

Antoninus Pius. Hadrian caused Antoninus to adopt two men as his sons and one of these in due course succeeded him—another highly conscientious and single-minded Emperor, Marcus Aurelius. He associated with himself as colleague his adopted brother L. Verus, who didn't count for much: indeed Verus achieved nothing till he roused himself to an effort and died of apoplexy.

So far the theory of the choice of the best man for the great duty of ruling had worked and worked well. Trajan, Hadrian, Antoninus Pius and Marcus Aurelius "maintained for more than eighty years a level of efficiency, devotion and common sense which, except for a few periods both rare and brief, had not been known since the death of Augustus."[15] But Marcus Aurelius had a son of his own, Commodus, and it is significant that as soon as ever a reigning Emperor had a son of his own, the free choice of the best man was replaced by the dynastic promotion of a son. It is just possible that Marcus Aurelius was so blinded by paternal affection as to believe that Commodus was the best man. If he did believe this, he enjoyed a monopoly of the belief. But the government was in Commodus' hands and those of his advisers, and there was no promising means of setting up a rival claimant even if a rival claimant could be found. The reign of Commodus showed what happened to the theory of government by the chosen best man if it was not, in fact, put into practice, that is if the best man was not chosen or the chosen was not the best man. The Principate had hitherto been governed in culture by the ideas of the fused civilization of Greece and Rome, and in politics it followed the ideas of Rome and, to some degree, of Greek philosophy adapted to Roman notions. Marcus Aurelius, who was at once a Stoic philosopher, a cultured gentleman, a devoted servant of his duties and an able and determined soldier, summed up in his person the best traditions of the Principate. His son Commodus may have been a mystic. If he was, that is the best that can be said of him. He broke with the old ideas and the old ideals and—to put it crudely—he let in the jungle. When he was murdered the throne was seized by an African soldier, Septimius Severus. The notion that the *princeps* was the chosen best man had passed—the Principate ends— and what has been called the Dominate—that is autocracy without political or ethical principles and based simply on military force—takes its place. The new alchemy produced not gold but iron.

With the end of the Principate we may properly look back to see how old ideas had changed their content with the times. In the first chapter I spoke of the two ideas of *dignitas*—the claim of the great man, and *libertas* the claim of the small man.[16] We have seen how the aristocratic concept of *dignitas* became more and more potent in the aristocratic age. It was something to which patrician nobles clung and something to which plebeian gentry aspired. Its satisfaction had been the most significant factor in the movement that led to the rise of the new nobility of office, which embraced patricians and plebeians alike; it was the characteristic of the leading senators, and it had a large share in producing the *auctoritas* of the Senate itself.[17]

One characteristic of most ancient aristocracies was the idea of equality within the ruling class. But, as has been observed, equality in the sense of parity of esteem was a notion which did not appeal to the realistic Roman mind. During the period of senatorial ascendancy the practice of this idea was in part preserved, although the Senate was hierarchic in its procedure. So long as the members of the senatorial Order could be satisfied by their steady progression to eminence, assisted by the virtual exclusion of newcomers, all went pretty well. But as the ascendancy of the Senate became less secure, what was at once a cause and an effect of this became visible in a more dynamic assertion of *dignitas*. Herein, as has been seen, lay a prime cause of revolutionary activity. There is what seems to be a genuine document in a letter in which Catiline justified his anarchical enterprise.[18] He declares in effect that, as he was denied the high place which belonged to him, he had to turn to violence to secure it. So too, when Caesar crossed the Rubicon he justified it to his troops by an appeal to his *dignitas*, which he called upon them to defend against his enemies.[19] With the advent of the Principate the *dignitas* of the nobles was gradually reduced to make way for the *auctoritas* of the *princeps*. It became less dynamic. If it was true that, as I have suggested, Caesar perished because his *dignitas*, at its height, took up too much room, now, after the great bloodletting of the civil wars the aristocracy was not so insistent on its *dignitas*. The idea becomes more diffused and less vivid in the decree about Vespasian to which I have referred earlier. This became apparent in the phrase "the *dignitas* of all things divine and human, public and private".

The obverse, as it were, of *dignitas* is *libertas*.[20] This claim—to do no more than the laws allowed but to suffer no more than the laws allowed—may well have inspired the creation of the Tribunes of the Plebs, for their first business was to bring help to men who claimed they were being oppressed. The traditional, if perhaps fictitious, figure of Brutus as the man who led the revolt against the Tarquins was, as it were, canonized as a *Liberator*, as his namesake doubtless remembered on the Ides of March. Meanwhile, in the world of foreign policy, the word *libertas* was used as a distinguishing mark of a city-state in contrast to an absolute monarchy, so that it assumed an almost diplomatic character. When Flamininus proclaimed the liberty of the Greeks, he was not conferring on the Greek cities any other freedom than the escape from the shadow of the Macedonian monarchy. In this Rome was more than half borrowing an idea that had found a place in the power politics of the Hellenistic age and even before it. Then it entered Roman politics in the age of revolution to arm both defence and attack in that field. And so, as may happen to words that are used in politics, it became a battle cry. And it was at home in civil war. And, as Thucydides has pointed out, when cities are visited by war and especially civil war, there occurs a kind of devaluation of words.

The famous account of his achievements which Augustus wrote and left behind him begins with the words: "When I was nineteen years old I raised an army on my own private initiative and at my own private expense, and by means of this army I restored to *libertas* the State which was crushed beneath the domination of a faction."[21] Caesar had declared in his *Civil War* that he left his province—this is a euphemism for the invasion of Italy—in order to restore to *libertas* himself and the Roman People crushed beneath a faction consisting of a few men.[22]

What kind of *libertas* did the State and the Roman People get? They got from Caesar an autocratic dictatorship. They got through the exertions of the young Octavian and his allies an autocratic Second Triumvirate. Liberty had become a political catchword—domination (*dominatio*) had come to mean political control exercised by your enemies. These are then described as few, which means that their claim to rule is not broad-based. But if it is a question of fewness three tri-umvirs were few and a single dictator was as few as few could be. So in the name of Liberty both sides seek to make their will prevail. The Liberty which Octavian declared he was restoring to Rome was figured in the type that was being struck on the coins of his opponents Brutus and Cassius. Both sides indeed declared themselves to be liberators—one from a tyranny, the other from an aristocratic clique.

Such was *libertas* in this special political sense during the time in which the control of the State, for whatever purpose, was the prize of victory. It does not mean that some of those who fought for it were not defenders of an ideal, but its ideals were strongly alloyed with the element of ambition. Then, when the Republic with its free competition for power had made way for the Principate and the Imperial regime was too strong to be challenged, *libertas* declines to one of two meanings: the first is a nostalgic memory of the Republic, the second, which is most clearly discernible in the writings of Tacitus, is the absence of servility, the maintenance of a man's self-respect, even if this is attended by danger to himself.[23]

Next there is the concept of *fides,* which had reflected the conscientious unself-regarding exercise of office or patronage in the Roman sense of the word.[24] Then with the advance of Roman power, especially in the second century B.C., the *fides* of the Roman People became something to which other communities appealed, to which, indeed, they subjected themselves. They did not always know what they were doing, and they sometimes found that the *fides* of the Roman People meant little more than that Rome could treat them as she thought fit, subject not to any rights they retained, for they retained none,[25] but only to whatever mercy Rome or some Roman general might show to them. And sometimes, as in her dealings with Carthage, the *fides* of the Roman People came nearer to bad faith than to good. The word belonged to the vocabulary of power and victory, and it might tempt to their abuse. (To take a parallel instance as an illustration: when the emperors.

were endowed in a special sense with the quality of clemency, the word had an ominous ring when it was an inclination to forgive in the mind of one who had an absolute and unchallenged right to be unforgiving.) To return to *fides*: this does not mean that, as between Romans or equals, *fides* did not retain its old meaning, but it was a poor protection to the weak and the alien. Then when power comes to be monopolized by the head of the State, *fides* becomes loyalty and even obedience. So, for example, Imperial coins[26] display the legend of the *fides* of the army or of the armies, which means their abiding loyalty to the emperor, or possibly reflects an emperor's consciousness that the army might well be more loyal than it is.

To turn for a moment to *religio*. To the old ideas, now dim with age and partial disuse, was added under Augustus a tentative approach to ruler cult which, as time goes on, becomes an ever more widespread sentiment directed to the personality of the reigning *princeps*. Millions of people who had never seen Rome or a Roman emperor, who knew nothing of Roman politics or Roman constitutional forms or doctrines, made prayers for the health of the emperor and they put the statues of emperors in their temples and they turned out in their best clothes to attend the ceremonies of the cult of good emperors who on their death had joined the gods, or the ritual which invoked the living emperor's *genius*, that is, his spirit. In this they expressed a common loyalty to the head of the Empire whoever he might be, and so usefully promoted a sense of the unity of the Empire.

Granted all this, there is something to be said in conclusion on what the Empire and the emperors now came to stand for among ordinary people under the Principate. They stood, above all, for Peace. When Napoleon III said "The Empire is Peace", he said, with less good grounds, what Augustus might have said.

And when the elder Pliny[27] spoke of "the measureless majesty of Roman peace"—*immensa Romanae pacis maiestas*—he was not indulging in hyperbole. Once the frontiers had been defensively advanced and made secure, there were either very few wars or only distant ones. But peace under the Principate received a positive content, something more than the absence of military operations. Peace came to mean more than that. It was not only freedom from the fear of war, it was the confident belief that men could live side by side in *ordered security*. And what in the eyes of Saint Augustine came from Heaven, in the eyes of the whole Empire of the Principate for more than two centuries came from Rome. From the time of Augustus to the time of Marcus Aurelius it was almost invariably true that men might pass securely by sea and land on their lawful occasions. If, for instance, some Syrian trader set out to go where business took him from his home town to Hadrian's Wall, he was sheltered by a strong hand and no one dared to make him afraid.

The converse of this was the belief that the emperor, whoever he might be, was what we might call an earthly Providence. This belief the emperors fostered partly by the constant suggestion found on the Imperial coinage, which suggested to the peoples of the Empire what they were to think about the regime of the moment. For this purpose the ancient world had no better medium than coinage, and it was probably an effective one. It had a kind of twofold appeal, to property and to faith. The more you had the emperor in your pocket, the more he had you in his. And the *providentia* of emperor after emperor is perhaps the most constant theme. In a masterly lecture on "The Virtues of a Roman Emperor",[28] Mr. M. P. Charlesworth said that what the ruler must persuade his subjects is first that he is fit to rule them, and second that they are being ruled for their own good.[29] To prove the first, that the emperor was fit to rule, it was sufficient to predicate of him the four cardinal virtues that adorned the golden shield of Augustus: virtue, clemency, justice and piety. And for the second, the keynote was *providentia*. This note is struck as early as Augustus, though softly and with a tactful gesture towards the Senate. At the beginning of one of the Cyrene decrees[30] Augustus writes, "I have decided to send a decree of the Senate to the provinces, so that it may be known to all *who are cared for by us*, and to append it to my pronouncement. From this it will be plain to all how much *care* I and the Senate take to prevent any of our subjects suffering unjust treatment or extortion." That is one side in its beginning; and this idea grows and grows till it reaches a climax with Hadrian and the Antonines. But there are other facets to *providentia* besides the present far-reaching care of the *princeps*. There is the idea that this same quality causes him to look ahead, and his *providentia* is linked with the idea of the *aeternitas* of the Roman People and, more nearly, with the care for the succession.[31] The *pax Augusta* which had shielded the Empire from external wars is reinforced by the *providentia Augusta* which makes peace a boon to all subjects and seeks to protect them from that fear of civil war which was so potent an influence in making the Principate welcome. In these ideas there is, I think, to be found the spiritual background of the New Order, the very ideas which, before the autocracy of the Dominate supervened, brought so much continuing happiness to the human race.

NOTES

I. EARLY ROME

1. See H. Last in *Camb. Anc. Hist.*, VII, 347.
2. viii, 86 ff.
3. "Placidi pellacia ponti". ii. 559; cf. v. 1004–5.
4. Virgil *Aen.* viii. 638; Horace *Odes* iii. 6, 39; *Epod.* 2. 41; *Epistles* ii. 1. 25; Ovid *Am.* ii. 4. 15; Propertius ii. 32. 47.
5. U. von Lübtow, *Das römische Volk, Sein Staat und sein Recht* (Frankfurt: Klostermann, 1955), pp. 17 ff.; E. Kornemann, *Römische Geschichte* (Stuttgart: Kröner, 1938), I, 50 ff.
6. F. Liefer, *Die Einheit des Gewaltgedankens im römischen Staatsrecht* (Munich: Duncker-Humblot, 1914); Ernst Meyer, *Römischer Staat und Staatsgedanke* (Zurich: Artemis-Verlag, 1948), pp. 109 ff.
7. Last, *op. cit.*, VII, 384 f.
8. *Aen.* vi. 851.
9. E. Gjerstad, *Early Rome*, I. "Stratigraphical researches in the Forum Romanum and on the Appian Way". *Acta Inst. Rom. Regni Sueciae*, XVII (1952), II. "The Tombs", *ibid.*, 1956. See also other papers in *Bull. Comm.*, 1949–56; *Studies D.M. Robinson*, II (1951); *Opuscula Romana*, I (1954). For a criticism of these conclusions see A. von Gerkan, "Zur Frühgeschichte Roms", *Rhein. Mus.*, 100 (1957), 82 ff.
10. For a constitutional reconstruction along these lines see K. Hanell, *Das altrömische eponyme Amt* (Lund: Gleerup, 1946).
11. Von Lübtow, *op. cit.*, p. 26.
12. H. Last, "The Servian Reforms", *Journ. Rom. Stud.*, XXXV (1945), 30 ff.

13. For a comprehensive discussion of the phrase "res publica" to the beginning of the second century, see H. Drexler in *MAIA*, N.S. IV (1957), 247.

14. *De re publica* i. 39.

15. Meyer, *op. cit.*, pp. III ff.

16. Von Lübtow, *op. cit.*, pp. 39 f.

17. See below, p. 32.

18. See U. Knoche in *Gymnasium*, 59 (1952), 329, 331 f.; cf. A. Alföldi, *Mus. Helv.* 10 (1953), 122.

19. *De re publica* i. 39.

20. H. Wegehaupt, *Bedeutung und Anwendung von dignitas in den Schriften der republikanischen Zeit* (Ohlau im Schlesien: Eschenhagen, 1932); H. Drexler, *Dignitas* (Göttingen: Dieterich, 1944).

21. Ch. Wirszubski, *Libertas as a Political Idea at Rome,* etc. (Cambridge, Eng.: Cambridge University Press, 1950), pp. 7 ff.

22. vii. 33. 3: "haud minus libertatis alienae quam suae dignitatis memor."

23. On *fides* see esp. E. Fraenkel, "Zur Geschichte des Wortes *fides*", *Rhein. Mus.* 71 (1916), 187 ff.; R. Heinze, "*Fides*", *Hermes,* LXIV (1929), 140 ff.

24. "Uti ei e re publica fideque sua videretur"; cf. Meyer, *op. cit.,* p. 241.

25. This relation, with its reciprocal evocation of *fides*, means loyalty also in the sphere of politics. See below, p. 20.

26. See R. Heinze, "Auctoritas", *Hermes,* LX (1925), 348 ff.; Meyer, *op. cit.,* pp. 245 ff.

27. See R. Heinze, *Vom Geist des Römertums* (Leipzig: Teubner, 1938), pp. 281 f.

28. Von Lübtow, *op. cit.,* pp. 482 f.

29. *N. H.,* VII. 213–14.

II. THE GROWTH OF THE REPUBLIC

1. U. von Lübtow, *Das römische Volk, Sein Staat und sein Recht*, pp. 83 ff.
2. H. Last, "The Servian Reforms", *Journ. Rom. Stud.*, xxxv (1945), 30 ff.
3. Von Lübtow, *op. cit.*, pp. 87 f.
4. See A. Bernardi, "Dagli ausiliari del *rex* ai magistrati della respublica", *Athenaeum*, xxx (1952), 3 ff., esp. pp. 12 f.
5. J. Vogt, *Römische Republik* (Freiburg: Herder, 1932), p. 27.
6. Von Lübtow, *op. cit.*, p. 90.
7. For a criticism of the tradition see H. Last in *Camb. Anc. Hist.*, vii, 504 ff.
8. See p. 30.
9. Von Lübtow, *op. cit.*, pp. 92 ff. This protection took a religious colouring as well.
10. That this is what they had done can be deduced by comparison with what can be discovered of the content of earlier annalists. For that appears to be, for this period, a comparatively meagre story largely based on yet more meagre records and traditions.
11. "Romanzata ben più che ricostruita". P. Fraccaro, "La storia romana arcaica", *Rend. dell' Istituto Lombardo*, lxxxv (1952), 117. (*Opuscula*, i, 22.)
12. See A. Rosenberg, *Der Staat der alten Italiker* (Berlin: Weidmann, 1913).
13. K. J. Beloch, *Römische Geschichte* (Berlin: de Gruyter, 1926), p. 232; Von Lübtow, *op. cit.*, p. 175.
14. See "Consular Tribunes and Their Successors", *Journ. Rom. Stud.*, xlvii (1957), 9 ff. and the literature there cited.
15. Livy iv. 1–6; Dion. Hal. xi. 53–61.
16. Livy iv. 7. 2.
17. Beloch, *op. cit.*, p. 254.
18. *Journ. Rom. Stud.*, xlvii (1957), 13.
19. By the Lex Hortensia of c. 287 B.C.

20. The reason for this limitation was presumably a practical care for military discipline. Von Lübtow, *op. cit.,* p. 103.

21. See above, p. 22.

22. See below, p. 34.

23. Last, *Camb. Anc. Hist.* VII, 537 ff.

24. In 232 B.C. See, for the advantages and disadvantages of the proposal, Tenney Frank, *ibid.,* VII, 806 f.

25. See literature cited by Kübler in Pauly-Wissowa, *s. v.* "Centuria", cols. 1956 ff.; E. S. Staveley, "The Reform of the Comitia Centuriata" in *Amer. Journ. Phil.* 74 (1953), 1 ff.; and J. Bleicken, *Das Volkstribunat der klassischen Republik, Studien zu seiner Entwicklung zwischen 287 und 133 v. Chr.* (Munich: Beck, 1955), pp. 33 ff.

III. THE AUTHORITY OF THE SENATE

1. The first instance was in 327 B.C. For the institution, see *Camb. Anc. Hist.* VII, 530 f.

2. See above, p. 33.

3. See K. von Fritz, *The Theory of the Mixed Constitution in Antiquity* (New York: Columbia University Press, 1954), p. 174.

4. *Ibid.,* 177 f.

5. As time went on, the Republic developed a kind of Civil Service (see A. H. M. Jones in *Journ. Rom. Stud.,* XXXIX (1949), 38 ff.) but not so organized or at such a level as to assist the making of policy.

6. See, in particular, H. H. Scullard, *Roman Politics 220–150 B.C.* (Oxford: Clarendon Press, 1951).

7. See above, p. 34.

8. See, for the evidence, J. Bleicken, *Das Volkstribunat der klassischen Republik, Studien zu seiner Entwicklung zwischen 287 und 133 v. Chr.*

9. *Ibid.,* pp. 68 ff.

10. Polybius vi. 3. On this concept, as on Polybius's treatment of the problem, see especially von Fritz, *op. cit.*, Chaps. IV and VII.
11. Polybius vi. 16. See F. W. Walbank, *A Historial Commentary on Polybius* (Oxford: Clarendon Press, 1957), I, 691 f.
12. Polybius vi. 11 ff. See Walbank, *loc. cit.*
13. *De re publica* ii. 56. See on the general question M. I. Henderson "Potestas regia", *Journ. Rom. Stud.*, XLVII (1957), 82 ff.
14. Polybius vi. 15.
15. By Cineas, Chancellor and envoy of Pyrrhus. Plutarch *Pyrrhus* 19; Florus i. 13.
16. For an instance see Cicero *Ad fam.* viii. 8. 6 ff.
17. Livy xxi. 63. 3.
18. H. Hill, *The Roman Middle Class in the Republican Period* (Oxford: Blackwell, 1952), pp. 50 ff.
19. See M. Gelzer, "Nasicas Widerspruch gegen die Zerstörung Karthagos", *Philol.* XL (1931), 261 ff., esp. 272 ff.
20. See above, p. 28.
21. See "Delenda est Carthago", *Camb. Hist. Journ.* VIII (1946), 117 ff., esp. 127 f.
22. See above, p. 50.

IV. THE AGE OF REVOLUTION

1. The re-election of tribunes was not without ancient precedent and was almost certainly not barred by statute. Some at least of the reasons against the re-election of magistrates did not apply to the tribunate. But custom was against it: it had become "a half-forgotten expedient of an age that was now remote" (H. Last in *Camb. Anc. Hist.*, IX, 33, where may be found a judicious discussion of the question).
2. See Last, *ibid.*, p. 35.
3. By the intervention of Scipio Aemilianus. See Last, *ibid.*, pp. 42 ff.
4. The Lex Acilia. For what remains of this plebiscite see *Fontes iuris Romani antejustiniani*, I² pp. 84 ff.

5. The condemnation of P. Rutilius Rufus in 92 B.C. See Last, *op. cit.*, pp. 175 ff.

6. For two instances cited by C. Gracchus, see Malcovati, *Frag. Or. Rom.* II, 140 f.

7. For a full discussion of the *Senatus Consultum Ultimum*, see Last, *op. cit.*, pp. 83ff.

8. The efforts of the tribune M. Livius Drusus to solve the problems of the day by reforms proved abortive, but this was in a large measure due to the injection of the Italian Question into domestic politics. Otherwise a workable compromise between the Senate and *equites* might have given stability to the convention of senatorial government.

9. As at the time of Cicero's recall from exile in 57 B.C.

10. See A. N. Sherwin-White, "Violence in Roman Politics", *Journ. Rom. Stud.*, XLVI (1956), 1 ff.

11. See H. Strasburger in Pauly-Wissowa, *s. v.* "Optimates".

12. It follows from this that some Roman politicians might act more as *populares* one day and more as *optimates* another, especially those whose family traditions did not commit them in advance. On earlier developments of the *popularis* tradition see M. I. Henderson in *Journ. Rom. Stud.*, XXXI (1941), 177.

13. For the course of Roman politics in the later part of the revolutionary period see, in particular, L. R. Taylor, *Party Politics in the Age of Caesar* (Berkeley, Calif.: University of California Press, 1949), and R. Syme, *The Roman Revolution* (Oxford: Clarendon Press, 1939).

14. Certare ingenio, contendere nobilitate,/noctes atque dies niti praestante labore/ad summas emergere opes rerumque potiri. ii. 11–13.

15. The over-all failure of repeated attempts to restrain bribery is one symptom of a deep-seated evil at this time. See R. E. Smith, *The Failure of the Roman Republic* (Cambridge, Eng.: Cambridge University Press, 1955), pp. 123 ff.

16. *Ad Att.* ix. 10. 2.

17. See on this R. E. Smith, *Service in the post-Marian Roman Army*

(Manchester: Manchester University Press, 1958), Chaps. II–IV.

18. See H. Strasburger, *Concordia Ordinum* (Frankfurt: Noske, 1931).

19. See Ch. Wirszubski, "Cicero's *Cum Dignitate Otium*: a Reconsideration", *Journ. Rom. Stud.*, XLIV (1954), 1 ff.

20. See R. Heinze, "Ciceros 'Staat' als politische Tendenzschrift", *Hermes*, LIX (1924), 73 ff.; R. Reitzenstein, "Zu Cicero *de re publica*", *ibid.*, pp. 356 ff.; K. Sprey, *De M. Tulli Ciceronis politica doctrina* (Zutphen: Nauta, 1928), pp. 253 ff.; W. W. How, "Cicero's Ideal in his *de Republica*", *Journ. Rom. Stud.* XX (1930), 24 ff; R. Meister, "Der Staatslenker in Ciceros *De republica*", *Wien. Stud.*, LVII (1939), 57 ff.

21. Suetonius *Div. Iul.* 77.

22. *Camb. Anc. Hist.*, IX, 704 f.

23. For reasons in favour of this opinion, see *ibid.*, pp. 718 ff.

24. This general judgment is only slightly affected by Octavian's approaches to a more constitutional position from 36 B.C. onwards.

V. AUGUSTUS PRINCEPS

1. *Adventures of Ideas* (Cambridge, Eng., 1933), p. 56, quoted by H. Last in *Journ. Rom. Stud.*, XXXIV (1944), 119.

2. Almost all the most eminent posts in the provinces and the armies were held by senators. On the position of the Senate in Rome see below, p. 83.

3. It is true that, as an Order, they ceased to be a political force and lost most of their financial opportunities at Rome itself, but the patronage of the *princeps*, and the economic progress which the Principate secured, were a more than sufficient compensation.

4. On Agrippa see especially M. Reinhold, *Marcus Agrippa: A Biography* (Geneva, N. Y.: Humphrey, 1933), and R. Daniel, *M. Vipsanius Agrippa* (Breslau: Marcus, 1933).

5. See Pauly-Wissowa, *s. v.* "Maecenas", cols. 209 ff.

6. *Res Gestae* 34. 1. See *Class. Quart.*, XLV (1951), 130 ff. This conjecture is based upon the exegesis of this passage. It is not attested elsewhere, and it is possible that Augustus' memory was not precise.

7. This must be the meaning of the word *arbitrium*, and it suits Augustus' technique and personality.

8. M. P. Charlesworth, "The Virtues of a Roman Emperor: Propaganda and the Creation of Belief". *Proc. Brit. Acad.*, 1937, pp. 105 ff., esp. pp. 111 ff.

9. On the meaning of *imperium maius* see especially J. Béranger, *Recherches sur l'aspect idéologique du principat* (Basel: Reinhardt, 1953), pp. 74 ff.

10. Last, "*Imperium maius*", *Journ. Rom. Stud.*, XXXVII (1947), 157 ff., esp. 163 f.

11. *Camb. Anc. Hist.*, X, 138.

12. The *cohortes urbanae* would serve this purpose, and in A.D. 6 the *Vigiles* as part of their duties.

13. Tacitus *Ann.* i. 2. 1: "ad tuendam plebem tribunicio iure contentum"; cf. iii. 56. 2.

14. *Camb. Anc. Hist.*, IX, 900 f.; E. Hohl, "Besass Cäsar Tribunengewalt?" *Klio*, XXXII (1939), 61 ff.

15. On this possibility (Dio Cassius liv. 10. 5) see A. H. M. Jones, "The *imperium* of Augustus" in *Journ. Rom. Stud.*, XLI (1951), 112 ff.

16. *Res Gestae* 34. 3; on the meaning of the word 'quoque' and of the phrase in general see *Journ. Rom. Stud.*, XLII (1952), 10 ff.

17. See below, p. 84.

18. See above, p. 47.

19. See Pauly-Wissowa, *s. v.* "*Princeps*", cols. 2014 ff.

20. See above, p. 47.

21. See Last, "Imperium maius", *Journ. Rom. Stud.*, XXXVII (1947), 163 f., and XL (1950), 121 ff.

22. See E. T. Salmon, "The Evolution of Augustus' Principate". *Historia*, V (1956), 456 ff.

23. Tacitus *Ann.* i. 3. 7.
24. Suetonius *Div.Aug.* 28. 2. See W. Weber, *Princeps* (Stuttgart: Kohlhammer, 1936), I, 27 ff. for a commentary on these words.
25. *Res Gestae* 35. 1; cf. Cal. Praeneste to Feb. 5. Ovid *Fasti* ii. 127–28; Suetonius *Div. Aug.* 58.
26. The literary connotations of the phrase (see A. Alföldi, "Die Geburt der Kais. Bildsymbolik", *Mus. Helv.* 10 [1953], 117 ff.) may, however, point to what would be this more esoteric interpretation.
27. Charlesworth, *op. cit.,* p. 107.
28. On this much disputed question see E. Schönbauer, "Wesen und Ursprung des röm. Prinzipats", *Zt. Sav. Stift. rom. Abt.,* XLVII (1927), 264 ff. esp. 310 ff.
29. See G. Tibiletti, *Principe e magistrati repubblicani, ricerca di storia augustea e tiberiana* (Rome: Signorelli, 1953).
30. See below, p. 103.
31. The ancient evidence for Augustan ruler cult is clearly set out by H. Heinen in *Klio,* XI (1911), 129 ff.
32. A. D. Nock in *Camb. Anc. Hist.,* X, 485.
33. *Ibid.,* pp. 483 f.
34. *Ibid.,* p. 487.

VI. THE DEVELOPMENT OF THE PRINCIPATE

1. For a full statement of the evidence for the succession to the Principate see L. Wickert in Pauly-Wissowa, *s. v. "Princeps",* cols. 2137 ff.
2. As *principes iuventutis.* See *ibid.,* cols. 2299 ff.
3. L. Caesar (b. 17 B.C.) died in A.D. 2; C. Caesar (b. 20 B.C.) died A.D. 4.
4. His will began with the words "Quoniam atrox fortuna Gaium et Lucium filios mihi eripuit" (Suetonius *Tib.* 23). Cf. *Res Gestae* 14. 1.
5. Tacitus *Ann.* i. 11. 1–2.

6.   *Ibid.*, i. 6–14.

7.   See M. P. Charlesworth in *Camb. Anc. Hist.*, x, 652.

8.   *Ibid.*, pp. 668 f.

9.   *Fontes iuris Romani antejustiniani*, I², 154 ff.

10. See H. Last in *Camb. Anc. Hist.*, xi, 407 f.

11. *Ibid.*, p. 403.

12. Suetonius *Div. Vesp.* 25.

13. *Panegyricus* 7. 6.

14. *Agricola* 3.

15. Last, *Camb. Anc. Hist.*, xi, 413.

16. See above, p. 13.

17. See above, p. 39.

18. Sallust *Bell. Catil.* 35.

19. *Bell. Civ.* i. 7. 6.

20. See above, p. 13.

21. *Res Gestae* 1. 1.

22. *Bell. Civ.* i. 22. 5.

23. Ch. Wirszubski, *Libertas as a Political Idea During the Late Republic and Early Principate*, Chap. 5, esp. pp. 160 ff.

24. See above, p. 13.

25. This was the legal effect of *deditio*. See P. de Francisci, *Storia del diritto romano* (Rome: Anonima Romana Editoriale, 1926), I, 291 and A. Heuss, "Die völkerrechtlichen Grundlagen der röm. Aussenpolitik in republ. Zeit", *Klio Beih.*, xxxi (1933), 62 ff.

26. See e. g. Mattingly-Sydenham, *Roman Imperial Coinage* (London: Spink, 1923), I, 229–31; II, 276, 295.

27. *N. H.* xxvii. 1. 3.

28. See *Proc. Brit. Acad.*, 1937, pp. 110, 115.

29. *Ibid.*, p. 108.

30. Edict v. 11. 77–82.

31. See M. P. Charlesworth, "Providentia and Aeternitas", *Harv. Theol. Rev.*, xxix (1936), 107 ff., esp. 117 ff.

INDEX